Nancy V

SOUTH AFRICAN WINTER

SOUTH AFRICAN WINTER

by

JAN MORRIS

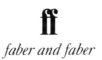

faber and faber

This edition first published in 2008
by Faber and Faber Ltd
3 Queen Square, London WC1N 3AU

Printed by CPI Antony Rowe, Eastbourne

A CIP record for this book is available from the British Library

ISBN 978-0-571-24731-8

ACKNOWLEDGEMENTS

This book owes its existence to the generosity of the *Manchester Guardian*, whose editor and proprietors sent me to South Africa and later allowed me the leisure to write it. The opinions it expresses are, of course, my own (or at least, since I am a wandering journalist, of my own distillation).

Besides thanking innumerable friends and informants in the Union, I must acknowledge with admiration the three books I myself found most useful in trying to understand the country: Dr. de Kiewiet's *The Anatomy of South African Misery*; *Drum*, by Anthony Sampson; and Alan Paton's *South Africa and Her People*, which is written primarily for children, but which contains a masterly summary of the conflicting views on race.

CONTENTS

ILLUSTRATIONS

MAP

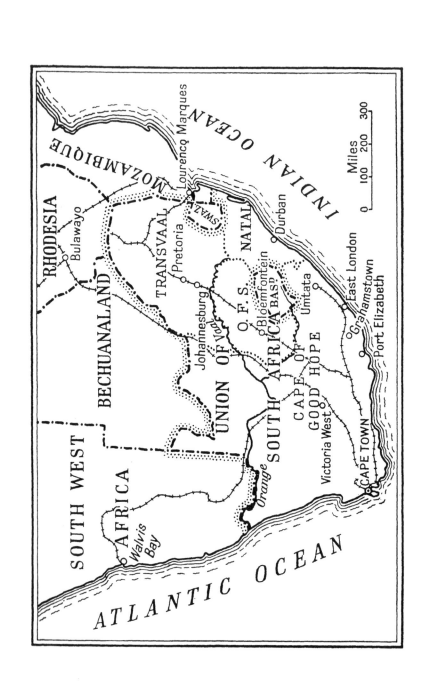

INTRODUCTORY

As a man is sometimes marked by the panoply of his profession, and a woman by the radiance of affection, so the States of the earth have their auras too: golden for Greece, garden-like for Italy, bear-skinned for Britain, jazzy but bespectacled (like a Kiwanis) for the United States of America. The darkest and most universally disliked of these miasmas surrounds the Union of South Africa, the strongest country of the African continent, and proclaims her something special among the nations: an outcast, a pariah, a skeleton in the upstairs cupboard.

In the African winter of 1957 I spent some months trying to penetrate this particular lamina, to delineate the national features that lay beneath and determine whether poor South Africa was as evil as her reputation. The country was then doubly disunited. The three million whites were bitterly divided among themselves, Afrikaner against English, with the Afrikaner Nationalist Government rampantly in control; and the Europeans as a whole were in desperate conflict with their ten million black and brown cohabitants. While the squabbling whites tried hard to maintain their positions and privileges, the voteless blacks were pressing ever more angrily for political rights and equal opportunities. Things seemed to be approaching a climax. The Nationalist policy of apartheid, or racial separateness, was being heartlessly enforced, and step by step the country was forcibly split into watertight compartments of colour. *Slegs Blankes*—'whites only'—was the text of the South African sermon in 1957; and its sacraments were the racial laws which, clause by clause, lash by lash, relentlessly forced the peoples apart and alienated them one from another. Elsewhere in the

13

world the black, brown and yellow peoples were storming into their own again: but in South Africa the political *status quo* was being deliberately maintained, as in a vice, by the policies of the State. The native must keep his place. White blood must not be sullied. The Europeans must not be swamped. '*Il ne passeront pas!*' cried the Nationalists, not without courage, as they manned the barricades against history, the black man and a hostile world.

Not every white South African supported the philosophies of plain apartheid. Some were visionaries, and had conceived the idea of autonomous African States within the present borders of the Union. Others, more bestial, stood frankly for baaskap—'boss-ship'—that is to say, white supremacy for ever. Many members of the English-speaking United Party, the official Opposition, advocated gradual progress towards racial equality, so gradual, indeed, as to be almost imperceptible except to themselves. Many more accepted Cecil Rhodes's classic dictum, 'a vote for every civilized man'. The Communists, and some adherents of the brave little Liberal Party, professed to believe in immediate political emancipation for everyone; and so apparently did the leaders of the African National Congress, the organ of the African risorgimento.

Colour was not the only problem besetting the Union that winter. There was the tedious conflict between the impotent English and their Afrikaner rulers; there were South Africa's difficulties in international relations, and the unsatisfactory price of gold, and the hardships of the investment market, and the perennial dangers of erosion and overstocking and drought. But the question of race dominated my visit, and inevitably infests the pages of this book. Exponents of every conceivable view poured their opinions into my ears as I wandered through the four provinces. Fanatics and cranks of every persuasion belaboured me with theories. When I began my journey, almost every viewpoint seemed reasonably plausible; half-way through I found myself suffering from a chronic condition of *déjà vu*; and when at last I left the Union all those eager advocates sounded equally threadbare and unconvincing, so tediously obsessive is

14

the subject of race in South Africa, so merciless the pressure of politics, and so infinitely distant a solution to the national difficulties. As on a drab treadmill, conversation in South Africa revolves endlessly round and round the black man, what his future is to be, whether we can trust him, how we should approach him, what we ought to do about him, how he smells, how delightful he is, how awful he is, whether we should allow our daughters to marry him, how we would like to have him living next door, whether we should shake hands with him, or sit by his side, or whip him, or give him the vote, or educate him, or pay him better, or sleep with him: until that sad symbolic figure, *homo Africanus*, looms constantly over the dinner-table and the coffee-shop like a harpy or a sculptured Moor.

For at the bottom of apartheid lies fear, an emotion you cannot dismiss with sophistries or exorcise with moral dissertations. This book offers no answer to the South African dilemma, because I know of no antidote to fear. I am sure that apartheid is the wrong solution, if only because it treats men not as individuals but as ciphers; but I learnt of no alternative that could bring tranquillity to black and white alike. We can hope for a change of heart among the rigid Afrikaner zealots, the shock troops of racialism; we can wish for the emergence of some moderate African leaders of genius; we can keep our fingers crossed for compromise rather than revolution; but if we feel like praying about it all, we must be frank with the Almighty, and ask for a miracle.

Such a book as this cannot ignore these terrible conundrums, any more than I could. But do not be alarmed. It is not all politics. Cheerfulness keeps breaking in.

1

WHITE JOHANNESBURG

It is sad but fitting that the northern gateway of the Union should be the swollen mining-camp of Johannesburg, the most miasmal of the South African cities. Greedy, harsh and angular, it stands on the bleak uplands of the High Veldt like a totem of materialism, an unfailing confirmation of the traveller's preconceptions. You expect the worst of South Africa; and sure enough, as your aircraft flies in from the genial north, the grim landscape of the Witwatersrand lies there below you with an air of degraded melancholy, the least welcoming, the least jovial, the least heart-warming of countrysides.

Perhaps it is early morning when you arrive above the Rand, and a pall of mist and smoke and pale cloud hangs low over the country. Then there is an austere and bitter seduction to the scene. Far away over the veldt this vaporous carpet spreads sullenly, white and clammy; but protruding through its whiteness, giving an unworldly grandeur to the setting, stand the mine-workings of the Transvaal goldfields. The vast yellow mine dumps, flat-topped ziggurats, glisten a little in the early sunshine, the mist lapping their flanks. The big wheels of the mine-shafts revolve as the early shifts plummet to the gold galleries below. A solitary tall chimney smokes away on the horizon. In a sudden clearing in the vapour you may glimpse a train chugging through the suburbs to Boksburg or Springs: and away to the east, swirled and swathed in mist, there stand the tall cold buildings of Johannesburg. There is a dank beauty to this landscape, so sprawling and inhuman, a country nourished on gold: but there is nothing affectionate or soft about it, and nothing at all to calm your forebodings.

WHITE JOHANNESBURG

Nor is the city, when at last you arrive in your Volkswagen bus among its truncated skyscrapers, an immediately exhilarating place. It stands nearly 6,000 feet up, so that the guide books warn you not to be alarmed if you puff unduly on the stairs; and because it stands over a many-layered warren of mining tunnels it is sometimes gently shaken by earth tremors, the belly-rumbles of the Rand. But it has surprisingly little sense of pace or astringency. The publicists often speak of Johannesburg as a little New York, but here there is none of the sparkle, the dazzling colour, the sophisticated gusto of Manhattan. Jo'burg (as even its inhabitants call it) is more like one of the medium cities of the Middle West, perhaps Omaha or Grand Rapids, except that the shops are not so good. It sometimes feels painfully raw and new. Seventy years ago it simply did not exist, and until 1947 a familiar habitué of Pritchard Street, one of the principal streets of the metropolis, was the Mr. Pritchard it was named after.

Oddly enough, although Johannesburg is the world's greatest gold city and a business centre of incalculable importance, there is something rather haphazard to its arrangements. The streets are geometrical and orderly of design, but there is a peculiar tatterdemalion feeling to its traffic and wandering crowds. The white people feel oddly shiftless and flabby; and the myriad blacks lounge among the back streets, or saunter among the shops, or hurry towards their buses, or ride their bicycles with precarious indecision, giving the place a sort of crumbling black patina. Everyday life in Johannesburg is often snarled with unexpected petty difficulties. In the coffee-shop there seem to be far too many waiters trying to find the sugar all at once. At the bank there is likely to be some confusion about your telegram. The post office hasn't got the right form. The young man who tells you the way to the City Hall does so with endless imprecisions and contradictions, less like a city businessman than one of those circumlocutory country butchers whose opinions one sometimes rashly invites in looking for demure tree-shaded hamlets in Kent. Bite and decision is strangely lacking from the Johannesburg atmosphere, for all the cutting winter winds that howl down its canyons, and for all the calculating generations of skill that have secured its prosperity.

Gold is its life-blood, and even in the centre of the city you cannot escape the presence of the mines. Sometimes you may see, gazing blankly into a haberdasher's window, a black miner still wearing his mining helmet, like a soldier on week-end leave from the trenches: and as you wander about the streets you will often glimpse the alien mass of a mine dump, a yellowish mountain of waste, blocking the end of a thoroughfare or looming over the warehouses. Sometimes the colours of these dumps shift subtly in the sunshine; sometimes they glitter suddenly, as if minute particles of gold still embellished them, like rhinestones on a dowdy frock. There is talk of building a hotel on top of one of them, and others are being ransacked for unsuspected minerals (they are impregnated with arsenic, which, though convenient for murderers of mothers-in-law, hampers other schemes for their exploitation): but in general they look cool, aloof and neglected, with a massive Pharaonic beauty. There are a few gold-rush buildings in Johannesburg, too, ornate empillared stores or rambling hostelries, with a hint of the hitching-post and the frontier moll; and downtown there stand in blank grandeur the offices of the Anglo-American Corporation, the greatest mining corporation on earth. No sign relieves the austere magnificence of these offices, or softens their monolithic effect: only the magical words '40 Main Street' stand there as an imperial motto, the *Ich dien* of gold mining. Gold keeps Johannesburg powerful and boisterous, and the paving stones of its streets are, so the analysts swear, literally impregnated with gold dust.

Jews and hard-headed British money-men dominate the finances of this city. The times are bad, and the Stock Exchange is limping sadly, harassed by strong investment markets abroad and crippled by the reputation of apartheid. But there is still an agreeable speculative undercurrent to the conversations of Johannesburg. I once spent an evening with a minor millionaire in his pent-house flat, in the padded upper stories of one of his hotels. A small fountain played frigidly in the roof-garden and the drawing-room was rather self-consciously opulent. As we

19

sat there over our brandy my host tinkered nostalgically with his memories of Johannesburg's frothy financial past. He told me dreamily of many a long-forgotten manipulation, of strange ephemeral companies, of fortunes grandly gambled away, of old friends in prison or unaccountably at large, of marvellous intuitions and opportunities lost.

'So Eddy asked me straight, you see—I didn't know what he was up to, not yet. "What would Oppie do?" he said. I said, "get out there and buy Corner House." So I rang up four or five brokers—they knew me well, see, they knew I *knew*, and I said, "I want fifteen thou. for somebody very very important," and believe it or not, when I went round to my club that evening, a very old friend of mine said, "Bob, take a tip from me, buy 'em, what's good enough for Oppie should be good enough for you!" Ah, that was the real Jo'burg, boy, that was the real McCoy!'

With such obscure, and indeed sometimes apparently meaningless reminiscences, shot out of the corner of his mouth as a bookie shoots the odds, this anecdotal millionaire strolled up and down his splendid carpets, revolving his brandy-glass in his hand, emphasizing his points with the tip of his cigar, living again with infinite relish some of Mammon's greater holidays. I sat there entranced, for I had to admit that, Oppie or no Oppie, and despite occasional blurred references to hard labour and obloquies, it all sounded the greatest fun.

Few cities are more intimately adapted to the making of money. In its boom periods the whole white population follows the stock markets as keenly and as knowledgeably as ever a Londoner followed a Test Match. Johannesburg has a determined social life, a host of charitable organizations, and some vestigial public culture (the public library is splendid); but generally it is frank enough about its aspirations. There is a strangely compelling fascination to the steely hardness of the city, something complete and functional; and there are perhaps no suburbs in the world more brazenly comfortable than the magnificent white highlands on the northern edges of the city. They say that the white South African has the highest standard of living on earth; they assure me that the parliamentary constituency of

WHITE JOHANNESBURG

Hillbrow, in Johannesburg, is the richest in the British Commonwealth; and if you take an aeroplane over these wealth-sodden dormitories you will see the swimming-pools glittering there below you in their hundreds, among the smooth lawns, the tailored trees, the occasional bashful mock-Tudor and the grand modernistic flats. Less than a century ago there was not a single tree upon the site of Johannesburg: to-day the city is encouched in the gardens and greeneries of these fortunate suburbs. A swift procession of American cars sweeps along their avenues. At St. John's School, when the lunch bell rings, the small boys come streaming out in caps and shorts like an army of juvenile stockbrokers, as richly English as a five-pound note except for some indefinably South African foreshortening of their features. The Bishop of Johannesburg stands bravely in his purple cassock in a world of sprinkled lawns and cocktail dresses. Conversation is often excellent, for the rich people of Johannesburg are, by and large, an intelligent and perceptive lot; and often and again you may meet the author of one of those innumerable South African novels whose titles get embarrassingly jumbled into the brain, and whose plots seem to dove-tail easily into a kind of liberalistic, inter-racial, progressive, Book-of-the-Month-Club *mélange*. 'Of *course* you've read her book!' says your hostess with an expectant smile: but by Heavens, you can't for the life of you remember.

There is a parallel element of gaunt power to Johannesburg. If you stand on a ridge outside the city, on the stark rocky plateau of the veldt, you can see its big buildings elevated above the desert of the mine dumps with a squat and ugly force. There is little delicacy or elegance to the place—even the big stores smack heavily of the provincial draper, so that the dreariest of nightdresses stand in flat-chested modesty in the windows, and you almost expect the change to come churning overhead in one of those antique aerial cylinders. But a streak of brutal virility enlivens the city's ambiance. The great new railway station sprawls across the heart of the place, an enormous splodge among the office blocks. The City-Hall flaunts smoky, swing-door suggestions of Tammany or Mayor Prendergast. And when there is a rugby match at the big stadium the whole white population seems to be there, shouting its head off at the minutest nuance of technique or fortune, surely the most forceful sporting crowd of all.

The poorer Europeans sometimes reflect in their persons and manners a little of this stubby resolution. In the shabby white quarters that meander in and out of the mine dumps you may see them sitting on their stoeps, a leathery, open-necked kind of people. Some are British by origin, some Afrikaner, but when they talk English they share the peculiar flattened, twisted dialect that is the hall-mark of a South African. In some cities it is architecture that strikes the senses most forcibly; in others conversation; from some one remembers best the wail of a train whistle, the charm of a string quartet, the allure of a pink chiffon: but nothing can recall me more abruptly to Johannesburg than the memory of one of those pallid sentences, sing-song and hollow, that you hear wafted across a milk bar counter or eddying across a bus.

On my very first night in Johannesburg such a sentence found its way into my notebook. I was eating a depressed fried-egg sandwich in a snack bar in President Street. The night was cold, the street gloomily empty, and I was alone with the three middle-aged white-coated women who administered the shop. So violently distorted were their accents, and so bemused was I by the impact of the city, that I could scarcely understand a word they were saying to me: but one phrase did strike home. 'Man', said one of those ladies, sliding the salt across the counter, 'I can see by your face, you'll like Jo'burg so well you'll never want to go home again.' It did not seem probable to me, that draughty African evening, that her prediction would come true: but I confess to a sneaking, shamefaced affection for the Golden City, and a certain reluctant response to its magnetism.

2

TENSIONS

It is, though, a city chilled by a condition of appalling tension. White Johannesburg is lapped by another metropolis, the vast housing estates and slums of the segregated black locations: and every breath of its air is thick with the broodings of apartheid. Hate and suspicion are integral parts of the Johannesburg atmosphere. With the resentful African proletariat lying sullen about the city's perimeter, it sometimes feels like an invested fortress—except that each morning, very early, thousands upon thousands of black besiegers pour into the city to work. You are apart from the black men, and yet they are among you; you are afraid of them, yet you need them in your office or factory; you despise them, but you welcome their good hard cash in your till. Johannesburg is a schizophrenic city. Everyone knows that in those locations beyond the mine dumps terrible things happen when the sun goes down: the young tsotsi thugs go looking for adventure with their razor blades and loud ties; sozzled Africans brawl in their illegal drinking houses; there are gang wars and desperate tribal clashes and police raids and murders innumerable. A huge alien black world is on the move, just out of range of the neon signs.

This is a disturbing thought, even for the confident burghers of Johannesburg, and domestic life in the city is distorted by it. You must never leave your child alone with an African. At night you must shutter and bar your windows, set your burglar alarm and say your prayers with conviction. If you are especially apprehensive or resolute of chastity you may place a tear-gas bomb beside your face-cream on the dressing-table. If you are a millionaire in a pent-house flat you will prime the booby-trap

23

in your safe. 'I hope you don't sleep too heavily, sir,' said the housekeeper, when I arrived in Johannesburg. 'Your room's opposite the fire-escape, you see, and you never know who'll come creeping up, do you?' This chatty advice was supplemented by the eerie semi-silence of the Johannesburg winter night. After dark the city locks itself up, like a medieval stronghold dropping its portcullis, or a frightened Cairo merchant barricading himself against the plague. A curfew keeps the Africans at home. Few cars travel the streets, and there are hardly any of those loitering loving couples, or toothy prostitutes, or homely late-night buses, that give a comfortable geniality to the London midnight. Only the raggle-taggle black watchmen sit in their shop doorways, and sometimes they shout unintelligibly to one another, or sing a sudden snatch of song, or laugh throatily, or spit; and sometimes there are the sounds of a brief echoing struggle in an alley-way, pantings and choking imprecations, though when you reach the window in your pyjamas only the watchmen are still sitting there placidly, muffled in their old army greatcoats and their tattered balaclavas. Johannesburg never feels sound asleep: not because it is dancing, or loving, or putting the world to rights, but because its sleeping pills have lost their potency.

For this great city is a paradigm of the racial dilemma that obsesses half Africa and gives the Union its unenviable pride of leperhood. Here, better than anywhere else, you can pertinently ask the question: should the black man be westernized, or should he be encouraged to cherish his old African ways? Not only is Johannesburg a showplace of apartheid, the place where, above all, the new urbanized African is confronted by the entrenched privileges of the white man: it is also an intelligent city, where keen minds (and kindly ones, too) are constantly pondering the problem and searching for solutions. This is not a whole-hog white supremacy city. Somewhere among its money-bags there lies a conscience, and it is partly a sense of guilt that keeps it awake at night. In the grey classical buildings of Witwatersrand University, on a ridge outside the city, are to be found some of the least befuddled liberal thinkers in South Africa—

and both black men and white can study there, one of the three universities in the whole country where the student body is interracial. The broad-minded Institute of Race Relations lives in Johannesburg; there are many Jo'burg Jews of liberal inclinations; the *Star* is the best and most urbane newspaper in Africa; and in Commissioner Street are the offices of the magazine *Drum*, owned and edited by white men, but dedicated to the interests of the westernized African, and a most tenacious and effective enemy of apartheid. Johannesburg is a big city, with room for all sorts of faiths and deviations, and it is the undeniable capital of the new Africa, where the black crucible is being most furiously heated.

No wonder it is tense. There is an endemic revolutionary situation in Johannesburg, and from time to time it erupts into violence. Sometimes the African workers boycott the bus service as a gesture of their discontent, and come streaming into the city on foot, in their tumbledown second-class taxis, or in the cars of white sympathizers. Sometimes there is a half-cock attempt at a general strike, and you will find the hotels short of bell-boys, and only half the factory chimneys smoking, and an odd sense of desertion in the streets. The English-language papers are full of the awfulness of it all, and outside the Town Hall you may often observe a few tattered young liberal zealots, frowsy girls and stark young men, distributing pamphlets of protest and making your flesh creep. If ever a cabinet minister appears in Johannesburg, he will be attended by the matrons of the Black Sash, a women's organization which demonstrates its general displeasure with Nationalist policies by wearing black sashes and standing about in mournful silent attitudes at public events. The police of Johannesburg have a reputation for brutality; the courts are full of Africans arrested in their scores for failing to carry their passes or ignoring the curfew or procuring alcohol; and it is impossible to escape, in a conversation or a breakfast in bed with the newspapers or even a quiet stroll through the Sunday streets, the appalling antipathies of South Africa.

When I was in Johannesburg the most striking symptom of these anxieties and discontents was the queer 'treason trial' being conducted in the Drill Hall. One fine night the Government had swooped upon a variety of its opponents, flown them all to Johannesburg, and charged them with treason. All over the Union people were arrested without warning, some of them pulled harshly out of bed in the authentic Gestapo manner, and whisked into confinement. There were 156 of them. They were all members of prominent anti-apartheid organizations, and the Government's contention was that they were united in treasonable activity by a common thread of Communism. It was only a preliminary hearing at the Drill Hall that winter, and it might drag on for months, or fizzle out, or be frankly emasculated when it went to a higher court. The accused had been granted bail, and lived at home, or in the houses of kindly sympathizers; but each day they attended their mass trial at the Drill Hall, and on paper every one of them was liable to the death sentence.

This was one of the oddest and nastiest of African phenomena —and it did have an obscurely aboriginal flavour to it, as of recalcitrant chieftains dragged before their paramount ruler, or slaves examined *en masse* before their absorption by cannibal kings in Dahomey. The Drill Hall had been built in the old days of British South Africa. General Sir H. J. T. Hildyard, K.C.B., had laid its foundation-stone in 1903, and it had a low veranda, and lots of notice-boards, and a varnished brown orderly-room air. In this place the accused assembled each morning in attitudes of bored or truculent resignation. There was a suggestion of punch-balls and puttees to the big dun-coloured hall, a sort of leathery, gym-shoe smell, and a large notice above one door proclaimed incongruously: 'Escape Door: Not Locked.' The light was rather dim those cold winter mornings, and beside the entrance a policeman sat at a deal table holding his thriller up to the sunshine, the better to find some excitement in life.

This is one place in South Africa where racial segregation is tacitly abandoned. The audience is separated, to be sure, into the usual white sheep and black goats; but the accused are herded together hugger-mugger in their wire pen. Some are white, some are brown, some are proudly black. One or two read newspapers, some write letters, a few usually seem to be asleep.

TENSIONS

One man wears a green, yellow and black blazer. A tall elegant Jew sorts his colour slides with detachment; a young African girl, in a green beret and black-and-white flowered skirt, spreads her papers around her on the bench and works upon a thesis. Here a gay little Indian giggles with his neighbours, and here a lean, bearded black man, inexpressibly sinister of appearance, stares coldly at the ceiling like an upturned idol. Every shade of leftist opinion is represented here, sometimes in awkward proximity. The handsome black giant with the silver hair and the benign smile is Chief Luthuli, a great man of the Zulu people and the most remarkable black leader in the Union. That little white man with the foxy face is, in everything but name, an out-and-out Communist, and is indeed deep in *New Age*, the irrepressible organ of the neo-Communists. There are lawyers and clergymen and students and taxi-drivers and writers and wives and political activists: all are enemies, from one motive or another, of apartheid; all are opponents of the Nationalist Government; and all are, in theory anyway, candidates for the gallows.

South Africa is an odd amalgam of tyranny and liberty, about equally compounded: and to this strange hearing there is an unexpected element of old-school fairness. The magistrate is scrupulous; the police treat their prisoners kindly; there is something faintly academic or even recreational about the hearings. The Crown's evidence, presented by semi-literate plain-clothes detectives, is sometimes downright comic; one Presbyterian clergyman of Communist leanings, for example, is alleged to have been received by the Pope in audience 'at his church in Moscow'. The defence lawyers are often witty. When the court adjourns for its tea break, at eleven each morning, there is usually quite a cheerful atmosphere to the scene. Thermos flasks emerge from baskets. An eager African hawks group photographs headed 'Treason Trial, 1956', in which all this assembly sits in smiling rows giving the thumbs-up sign—the salute of African nationalism. The Presbyterian parson shows his neighbour the manuscript of next Sunday's sermon, already stamped with the cachet of the Special Branch censorship. The defence

27

TENSIONS

lawyers, who have volunteered their services, stroll among their clients or chat with Crown counsel (as they are still laughably called). A couple of reporters doodle at their table, and one or two Africans from the audience talk to their friends through the mesh of the wire. The unacclimatized visitor, fresh from the logicalities of Europe or America, feels his head whirl as he talks to a Zulu chief, a taxi-driver's wife from Durban, a rich Marxist lawyer, an Afrikaner police officer, and a schoolgirl from the audience in the gym slip and long black stockings of an almost forgotten England. Lear and Carroll would often feel at home at tea break in the Drill Hall.

But after a few moments we return ponderously to business. The police witnesses drone on, hour after hour, cliché after cliché. The girl goes back to her thesis, the Jew to his slides. Sometimes a defence counsel rises languidly to his feet. 'Your Worship, accused number 114 is in some stress. May she leave the court for a short time?'—and a short bespectacled African girl, biting her lower lip, gets up rather arrogantly and walks out of the compound past the spectators into the sunshine. An air of tired monotony settles upon the Drill Hall. Day after day, month after month, the treason trial drags on like this, and every morning has become very like another. It is part of the Johannesburg scene, like a long-running play on Broadway, or Madame Tussaud's. Nobody quite knows what its purpose is. Everybody agrees that it has an insidious Alice-in-Wonderland quality. But the South Africans have a brisk phrase for anything that is piquant or unaccountable in this city. They shrug their shoulders and they raise their eyebrows, and they take another bite at their buttered bun: 'That's Jo'burg!' they say with finality.

And if after a taste of this charade, you doubt the reality of misery in Johannesburg, stand outside that same Drill Hall in the evening, when the stores have closed and the factory hands are hastening out into the night. Then all the poor black workers of Johannesburg, forbidden to live within the precincts of the city, rush for the buses that will take them to their locations, to the slums or sprawling estates of the Western Areas. Each evening as dusk falls, and as the bitter night wind begins to whistle

28

through the buildings, a vast tattered queue moves in raggety parade towards the bus depot. It encircles the entire square outside the Drill Hall, so that the tail of the queue meets its own head, and all those thousands of Africans shuffle their slow way in double file towards their shabby buses. It is the longest, and saddest, and coldest queue I have ever seen. The bus service is frequent enough, and the black people do not usually have to shiver in the cold for too long: but there is an air of unutterable degradation to the scene, so heartless and machine-like is the progress of the queue, as the white folk hasten off in their cars to Hillbrow and Parktown, and the lights glitter in windows of the department stores, and these poor lost souls are crammed into their buses and packed off to their distant ill-lit townships. Many of them are half-starving. Most of them live in fear of robbery and violence when they step off the buses into the dark streets of the locations; half of them spend almost all their leisure hours travelling between the city and the far-flung patches of high veldt in which they are, by law, forced to live; they reach their homes long after dark at night, and they start for work again while the morning is still only a suggestion. You can hardly watch such a scene, and ponder its implications, and collate it with that dotty trial in the Drill Hall behind you, without the stirring of some crusading instinct, some Byronic impulse, or at least a stab of pity.

But when you get back to your hotel again, and are drowning the memory in a Riesling from the Cape, perhaps you will hear some tinny twangs of music from the street outside: and there beneath the arcades of President Street some solitary black man will be lounging by, in a tattered brown hat and blue dungarees, plucking away at a guitar as he walks, humming a high-toned melody, and expressing in his every gesture, in the very swing of his shoulders, the spirit of carefree indolence.

3

URBAN AFRICAN

For a queer mixture of pathos and vivacity characterizes the urbanized African of the Union. He is one of the most deliberately downtrodden men on earth, but he is also one of the most cheerful. He has lost the traditions and loyalties of his old tribal society, and lives in a wretched shanty-town or a soulless municipal location. His culture, such as it is, is a jazzy, mock-American, slangy kind of affair; and an African schoolmaster of some stature once told me that if it were not for the repressions and injustices of his life, the constant struggle against police and convention, he would feel his existence sadly lacking in stimulation. I spent a couple of days roaming around the Johannesburg locations in the company of Africans, and discovered that in their frustration they treated life under the shadow of apartheid as a kind of bitter game. We dodged the ubiquitous police cars for the fun of it, or in pursuit of some vague principle, rather than because we were at that particular moment breaking any particular law; and if the police questioned us, my friends planned to pass me off as a visiting doctor, called in to attend a wife suddenly crippled by some nameless disease. 'Natives Cross Here', said a notice beside the road, and my companions clapped me on the back and grinned: 'You see, man, we're just a lot of animals to them, like Beware of the Dog, or Please Don't Feed the Elephants. We're just a lot of animals in a zoo.'

Indeed at first the westernized inhabitants of these stark western areas did seem as strange to me, and as inexplicable in their manner, as queer laughing creatures in a menagerie. Their English is a strange muddle of Americanisms, Afrikaner idioms, and racy appendages of their own; but their manners are defiantly African. Sometimes they are grave and courteous, and you are reminded of Gold Coast chieftains or great men of the Congo; sometimes they treat you with such guileless flippancy that you think for a moment they are teasing you; sometimes a flash of malice enters their eyes, or something gives them such inexplicable amusement that they burst into a tumult of infectious laughter, or dance a little jazzy jig upon the pavement. When they talk, they do so with explosive animation; and when they listen, the whole of their being supplements their hearing, they become one great ear, and their white eyes, their tense bodies, their eager fingers and their yellow-striped socks all wait upon the speaker's words. There can be no better listener in the world than the Johannesburg African: however dull your story, however hesitant and ineffective your delivery, those big patient eyes will be fixed upon you with a gaze of infinite appetite and encouragement.

Most of the people I met in Sophiatown, Orlando, Meadowlands and the other famous African townships of the Rand had long since been detribalized. They owed no loyalties to Basutoland, Pondoland, the Xosa or the Zulu chieftains, but were men on their own, like the rest of us, commuting to the city each day and joining that desperate bus queue in the evening. One or two of them were prosperous, and had built houses to their own design, and owned cars and radiograms. Most of them were poor, and lived in little soulless homes slapped across the countryside by the authorities in endless monotonous rows. They were usually intelligent, if not fearfully reliable in small matters like punctuality and factual accuracy, and it seemed to me that in the abyss of their suppression their philosophies were agreeably devil-may-care. The way of the African in the Union is hedged by innumerable hard laws and impositions, designed to restrain the savage impulses of barbarians, but still applied indiscriminately to everyone, half-naked tribesman or gentle doctor. It is a crime to be impertinent to your employer, to leave your house without a pass, to strike, to enter a station by the European entrance, to be out of doors after curfew hours, to drink a glass of whisky without a permit. These laws are so patently unfair that they have long since lost any moral force. Most of the Johannesburg Africans go to prison some time in their lives; and they tell me that any African in the Union, arrested at any time and in any circumstances, could be successfully charged with some offence or other by any competent prosecutor. The police, mostly Afrikaners nowadays, are universally regarded as enemies. Laws seem made to be broken. The whole elaborate structure of repression has lost any claim to integrity. Some Africans work actively to change all this, to restore some semblance of dignity to their affairs. Most of them try to dance and sing and joke their way towards some ill-defined and unconvincing paradise. The hot-heads, educated to scorn the law, become tsotsis, gangsters and thugs of the most vicious kind. The more sensible spend their evenings in forbidden shebeens, drinking the liquor the law forbids them, dancing to the hilarious music of trumpets, hiding from the police (or corrupting them with alcohol), riotous, rhythmical and effervescent: as though the old Africa, with its drums and gorgeous colours, has come gaudily to the rescue of the new. The illegitimacy rate is dizzy. One African in twenty-four, somebody told me cheerfully in Sophiatown, can expect to be stabbed to death. There are witch-doctors in these vast townships; innumerable queer religious sects, with little gimcrack chapels and tottering wooden steeples; quacks and charlatans beyond count; thousands of jovial shebeen queens, ready to bury the brandy in the backyard when the police knock at the door; scores of jazz bands and choirs and dancing teams; clowns and preachers and angry politicians; and even a few writers and an artist or two, and a handful of scholars.

The intensity of life is often startling, like the vocabulary of the locations. As you drive round in your battered old car, innumerable passers-by will thrust their heads through the window, to exchange a few staccato greetings of slang with the driver and nod a welcome to you. Everyone seems to know everyone else, and to be privy to some secret joke, so that a wink or a grin or a shrugging of shoulders seems to serve as a benevolent password, and all is well. 'Pass, brother!' that snatch of rock 'n' roll seems to say, or that snaky wriggle of the hips, and so you rattle rumbustiously on, while the man beside you in the back seat explains how he once stabbed his Uncle Edward with a fork during an ill-considered fracas at a drinking den.

So there is colour and endless variety hidden below the drab surface of the locations, and sometimes there is also pride and dignity. In the condemned township of Sophiatown, one of the only three places in the Transvaal where an African may own freehold property, I once had lunch with a young African journalist and his wife. They lived in one room, but it was spotlessly clean and furnished with loving care. We heard both Mozart and jazz on a gramophone, and the food was excellent. In the courtyard outside a few scraggy hens picked at the rubbish, and a strange albino African child, all pink and red nakedness, stumbled here and there with a hoop; but inside all was kind and cultivated, and the wife looked after us with an almost Wordsworthian demureness, and the husband told me softly and without much rancour how much he wished to live as other men live, free and easy and preferably in America. Only a week or two before, he told me, there had been a police raid on a nearby district in the small hours of the morning; in one swoop more than a thousand Africans had been arrested for the pettiest of artificial crimes and carried away to judgment. 'Can you wonder we seem a little bitter sometimes, or drug ourselves with jazz and fooling?' I do not, as a rule, take easily to the company of Africans. Their temperaments are often alien to mine, and I have met few elsewhere on the continent with whom I could cherish intimate friendship; but in South Africa I met some who instantly mastered my loyalties, so kindly were their instincts, and so nobly (it appeared to me) did they face their misfortune. It seems an aeon and a million miles from these generous and civilized people to the hoop-la nationalists of Nigeria, the men who stand on one leg in the southern Sudan, or those poor stunted folk who wander around the markets of the Rhodesian copper-belt, picking their noses and buying hairy caterpillars for supper.

But to the masters of apartheid black men are black men, and

33

there's an end to it. For all their bounce and defiance, the townships of Meadowlands and Sophiatown, the shanty-slums of Orlando, Moroka, Pimville and Jabavu are the saddest places under the sun. Some of them are modern planned locations, some haphazard slums of hideous jumbled complexity, riddled with disease and squalor. Into this enormous complex of houses, huts and hovels, devoid of almost all the graces and comforts of urban living, 400,000 Africans are herded, as into a gigantic labour camp. Not long ago there was a substantial community of Africans in Johannesburg itself. Now the Nationalist Government has forced its black subjects farther from the Golden City, away from its swimming-pools and coffee-shops, into the harsh plateau of the veldt. One damp misty evening my African host stopped his car on a ridge above Meadowlands, and we surveyed in silence the expanse of African Johannesburg below us. As far as I could see, stretching interminably away into the dusk, the houses of the townships lay there blankly. A few candles flickered here and there (there is no street lighting, and no electricity) and a car or two moved urgently through the mist: but mostly the locations lay there torpid, numb and sullen. 'Our black metropolis!' said my host, with an ironic twist of his mouth. 'You see how they have cut us off? If there was any trouble they would isolate us here, this side of the railway line, and then bomb us and shell us until we surrendered.' I shuddered; he laughed, and clapped me on the back; and soon he left me at the door of my hotel, and the doorman looked at me queerly as his car rattled away down the street, back to the dim humiliations of Meadowlands.

It is the deliberate impersonality of the locations that is most terrible. In the modern housing schemes, excellent though they sometimes are, almost no variety, colour, or individuality is allowed. To be sure, Africans often erect their tribal huts in similar geometrical rows: but in Johannesburg you cannot escape the suspicion that this severe barrack-like order is intended to subjugate the African, to impress upon him his inferior status, to prove that he is not in white South Africa by right, but only on sufferance. He must never be allowed to feel a permanent resident, but must be branded as a migrant, a visiting servant whose only home is in his distant tribal territory. I know of few more dispiriting experiences than trying to find someone in a Johannesburg location at dusk: the roads bumpy and untarred, the constant fear of questioning policemen, the endless rows of dark identical houses, with numbers running up into the tens of thousands; the all-pervading sense of insecurity and mistrust; the vicious upland wind; the lights of Johannesburg shining mockingly in the distance; and the final moment of despair when at last you find the house, and knock at the door, and there emerges some demoralized sot in a grubby shirt and slippers, brandy on his breath, a flow of facetious speech tumbling over itself, and in the darkness of the parlour a blaring wireless and a half-eaten loaf. Poor African! snatched from his loyalties, his savageries and his tribal lands, deposited in helotry at 3467 North Kruger Road, he spends half of his life in recrimination, and the other half trying to be funny.

Less subtly depressing, perhaps, but more obviously gruesome, are the shanty-towns which have sprung up around the perimeters of the organized locations, a phenomenon of the South African industrial revolution. As the black men have flocked into the Rand to work in Johannesburg's factories, so they have outgrown their allotted locations; and there have appeared these huge tattered squatters' camps, made of old tins and corrugated iron and canvas and wooden boxes, like nightmare scouting camps, bursting with children and sunk in filth. In the summer they are blazing hot; in the winter a bleak wind howls through them, and the people huddle themselves in ragged blankets, or crouch over small fires like destitute wizards. Some of these camps have been there for twenty or thirty years, but they are as ramshackle and makeshift and threadbare as ever. Their latrines are open to the skies, surrounded by corrugated iron, and four or five men sit side by side in them, with no possibility of privacy. Urinals are simply buckets. 'But it's funny, this place makes me quite nostalgic,' said one of my guides, when we inspected one of these dismal installations. 'I grew up here, and when we were boys, whenever we saw a particular old

35

man come in here to the latrine we all used to follow him in, because he made such funny grunting noises. Every morning we followed him, man, all the whole lot of us like a procession, it was real funny to hear him!'

Among these sad communities there are several beer halls, licensed officially, where maize beer is sold at certain hours. One or two of these are new and spick and span; but the older ones look for all the world like cattle pens, into which, surrounded by corrugated iron and barricades, the black workers are put to sustenance. You can hear the clatter of these places far down the road, and smell the pungency of the fermentation, and as you approach you will be met by knots of half-inebriated Africans, singing and rolling. Thousands of men use these halls every day, and though the armed policemen at the door will not let you enter, you can see their black bodies in gaps between the corrugated iron, crammed and jostling, sitting at wooden plank tables or queueing with their tins for the beer. The noise, and the smell, and the congestion, and the sweat, and the sense of animal degradation is overpowering, and the beer (if you do manage to squirm inside) is awful.

There is a feeling of hopeless desperation to these locations, as if they have passed the point of no return. They are a symbol of all that has happened to the African in his pitiable attempts, now encouraged, now rebuffed, to master the white man's ways. At one end of the scale, new to Johannesburg, are the simplest of tribesmen, straight from the bush, dressed in blankets with exotic hats, still in thrall to magic and witchcraft and tribal ascendancies; at the other end is my young couple at Sophiatown, playing Mozart over their spaghetti and dreaming of New York. What can anyone do, short of some miraculous intervention, to sort out so terrible a muddle, drain such a reservoir of ill-feeling? Some of the white men who administer these locations are undoubtedly vicious and unseeing; but others seem to be playing parts in an inevitable drama, moved neither to pity nor cruelty, like insects that appear to feel no pain, or soldiers deadened by some terrible experience.

I went out to Orlando early one winter morning, before dawn,

to watch the progress of a strike. The African political leaders had called upon their people to stay away from work that day; the police had warned them that strikes among Africans were illegal; there was the possibility of violence. As the day broke I sat in the little police station, drinking sticky sweet coffee, and talked to the Afrikaner policemen who manned it. There was a sceptical officer with a Military Cross, and a big bluff Falstaffian sergeant, and a young sergeant-major with delicate hands; and we sat there in the cold and talked, and waited for something to happen.

'They'll go to work,' said the officer, 'you see if they don't. The trouble will start when they come back this evening, that's the time. The tsotsis will be after the poor bastards, and all these political boys. That'll be the time, after dark tonight.'

Then, suddenly turning to me, he said: 'You want to know something? I've killed four of these natives myself, with my own gun. They rioted down by the station, and started stoning and making hell, and I shot four of 'em dead, clean through the head.'

The sergeant-major coughed. 'And yet you know, sir, it's funny how much some of them can do, if you show them how. A Kaffir typed all of this lot'—and he showed me a list of names and figures—'yes, all by himself, once he'd learnt how. It's interesting how much some of them can do, really, if they get the chance.'

Once or twice the telephone rang as outlying stations reported. 'I thought so,' said the officer, going to the window, 'the poor bloody bastards are going all right. You can see 'em out here!' And there they were in the half-light, a few furtive figures scurrying towards the railway station, huddled in cold and fear.

'Of course,' said the officer pleasantly, pouring me another cup of coffee, 'you press people cause half the trouble. The way you write about things, you'd think these damned locations were in a state of revolution. I tell you, we've got 'em just where we want 'em. They can't move without us knowing. We know who the agitators are—and believe me (but you won't) we do our best to keep these poor bastards out of trouble. But we've got to keep our eyes open all the time, we've got to keep awake every minute of the damn day!' (It is always interesting to observe a conflict between emotions: and if ever you want to see a guilt complex at work, pick such a conversation with an intelligent Afrikaner policeman.)

As he spoke, and as the daylight began to creep grumpily through the windows, a man rushed in, panting and pale, and told us that there had been a train accident near the station. 'Damn!' said the officer: and at a run he led us out of the room and into the police cars waiting outside. 'Now you'll see the misery of it all,' said the sergeant-major, as we screamed down the road in the half-light: and he was right. It was raining and freezing cold, and the locations looked inexpressibly chill and friendless. A few Africans were hastening towards the railway line. From some of the little box-like houses women looked out with anxious faces. Others were as shuttered and lifeless as tombs. The accident had occurred on a high embankment, a place so rugged and exposed that if I turned my back on Orlando and shivered to the wind, and huddled my mackintosh about me, and looked at the harsh rock and coarse thin grass beneath my feet, I could imagine myself lost on an icy morning on some austere and unfrequented mountain-top. Two trains had collided, both of them full of Africans who had ignored the call to strike and were on their way to work. (They had European drivers, of course. An African may drive a train in the Congo or Ghana, in Nigeria or Equatorial France: but mercy, not in the Union!) The few casualties were being bandaged and taken away, and a track repair train was chugging in from Springs; but crouched around the wreckage, huddled beside the carriages or in little groups upon the railway line, the Africans stood ruminating in the wet, or talking in low undertones. 'This is the danger time,' said one of the policemen. 'If they're kept hanging around here for long, they'll begin talking among themselves, and then they'll flare up. God man, you haven't seen them when they start stoning! You won't soon forget it if they start this morning!'

Indeed, the atmosphere was ugly. The men and women all

38

around us looked surly and suspicious, and sometimes turning around suddenly, or raising my eyes, I would catch sight of a face staring fixedly at me with an expression of implacable distaste. 'Another half-hour of this', said the policeman, 'and somebody'll start whispering the Europeans arranged the crash, because of the strike. That's when the fun'll begin!'

All the miseries of South Africa seemed to fall upon us that morning with the drizzle. The rain teemed down upon us. The wind howled across the veldt, as though it would sweep all those myriad little houses down the hillside and away along a mud-filled gutter. The Africans around me were shivering; a respectable black woman in a feathered hat was sitting forlorn and bedraggled upon the railway line; the police and the cameramen bustled here and there; and all about us was the hot, unvoiced threat of a riot. This was the truth behind the vivacious façade of the locations: and sure enough, when at last the relief train arrived, and the passengers climbed sulkily into its bare carriages, I heard one middle-aged African say to his companion, in a flat, matter-of-fact tone of voice: 'Yes, but it didn't quite work, you see, because they meant to kill us all, every one of us. . . .'

4

PRETORIA

My most vivid memory of Pretoria, forty miles east of Johannesburg, is also tinged with African despair. I was driving out of the city early one morning to catch an aeroplane, and six or seven miles out of Pretoria I saw a black figure running helter-skelter down the road towards the city. A moment later another followed, and then two or three more: and they panted by us in a little raggety procession, with serious faces and bulging eyes, like participants in some strenuous sunrise celebration.

'What are they doing?' I asked my driver.

'Those Kaffirs? They're on their way to work. They've probably got to start at seven, and they've got a long way to go, so they have to run fast. It won't do them any harm.'

'You don't like Africans?' I said, subtly divining some such sentiment from his intonation.

'Kaffirs?' he replied with a genial twinkle. 'I love them like they was vermin.'

But this is not a predominant Pretoria tone of voice. This is the administrative capital of the Union, and it is a handsome, relatively chic little city, delectably set among hills and embellished with what a purist might consider a superfluity of jacaranda trees: that is to say, almost entirely submerged in them. (A Pretoria lady of resolution once grew so tired of the things that she walked outside her house with an axe and chopped down the nearest one in sight. It had been recently planted there by the municipality, one of a row of several hundred, and she was fined: but there is a wry humour to the Afrikaner, and within a week or two it had been replaced—by a lime.) I need hardly say that Pretoria is known in the guide-books and tourist offices

40

as The Jacaranda City: but, like the official description of Cleve-don as 'The Gem of Sunny Somerset', I suspect this has not passed very readily into the vernacular.

There is some fine architecture in Pretoria. On a commanding hill-side stand the Union's administrative buildings, designed by Sir Herbert Baker in one of his fits of monumentality, all scrolls and horsemen and classical façades; and there are one or two handsome modern structures, including a bank which offends the more strait-laced Afrikaners because it is decorated with nude statuary. ('Look how she stands there!' said one outraged citizen in a letter to the Press. 'In her uncovered nakedness she stands, with her legs wide, moreover with a stomach bared low and naked breasts, and the man's hand even over one bare breast. We must not allow the man and the woman to stand in that naked state and gaze upwards at the flag of South Africa!') Among the suburbs there are innumerable delightful ranch-style houses, all glass and imagination, in which well-to-do Pre-torians live lives of enviable comfort, and a noble complex of office blocks surrounds the City Hall. Nothing is ugly or squalid in Pretoria. The black people are tucked away in invisible loca-tions; the great steel works are only to be seen mistily in the distance; the diamond mines, where they found the legendary Cullinan, are twelve miles out of town; all is sweet and clean and Afrikaner.

This was the capital of the old Transvaal Republic, one of the two Boer States that defied the British Empire in the Boer War, and it is ennobled by the memory of President Paul Kruger, the supreme patriarch of the Boers, and the dour-faced imperturb-able generals who fought his battles so stubbornly. The war is the prime historical fact in the rather boring history of the Afrikaner nation, which seems to have consisted chiefly of inter-minable treks in ox-wagons, ferocious battles with black men, and an irresistible urge to be free from the shackles of inter-national obligation. There is thus an oracular quality to Pre-toria, and an air of battered sanctity surrounds the ornate but gloomy Raadsaal, seat of the Republican Assembly. In the centre of the city, the fulcrum of its emotions and its traffic alike,

'Oom' Paul stands himself, in an enormous posture of repose, wearing his celebrated top hat and with his back firmly to the railway station. Embattled burghers surround his plinth, and an intriguing (but erroneous) public legend has it that the inside of his hat is a bird-bath. His is not an immediately endearing figure. No uglier man ever lived, and an irreverent Afrikaner once suggested that a union between the President and Queen Victoria might have produced some memorable progeny. Here in Church Square, though, in the very heart of Afrikanerdom, there is an overpowering sense of pathos to his presence. The place is still alive with his memory, still reverberating with his proud platitudes. Here the irrepressible Boer commandos saluted him before galloping off on their ponies with their rifles waving and the biltong swinging from their saddles. Here the angry crowds assembled to demand the hanging of the Jameson Raiders, and here in the end the triumphant British ended the career of the republic and precipitated the President into exile. He may look rather comic, in his grotesque meditation above the square, but he has a home-spun magic to him still.

For Pretoria, despite its trimness, still expresses the sadness of a conquered capital. One night I sauntered through the town, beyond the grand office blocks, to the street where Kruger's house still stands in modesty. It was a warm and moonlit evening, with thunder in the air, and everywhere the people were sitting in their stoeps in their shirt-sleeves. A murmur of guttural Afrikaans accompanied me down the pavements. Crickets buzzed in the trees, a policeman strolled by whistling, the streetlights were soft and suggestive. It was like some small steamy, white-pillared town in the Mississippi Valley, where the dust tickles your nose and the honeysuckle incites your instincts. Against this unpretentious provincial background, so distant from the grandeurs of a Paris or a Washington, Kruger's house stood in demure melancholy, the most touching of national memorials. It is a little low house with a veranda, and two marble lions guarding its doorway: and on a rocking-chair beside the door Kruger used to sit and smoke and read his Bible, receiving his generals and petitioners cocking a snook at the

British, and accepting telegrams of goodwill from the Kaiser. An Afrikaner joined me as I stood looking at the house that evening, and we stood there for a moment silently in the light of the street-lamps. 'Oom Paul's house!' he remarked, with an explanatory gesture and the hint of an Oxford accent. 'One of our very best people, you know.'

For to this day this is how many of the Afrikaners see themselves: as a people of rocking-chairs and Bibles, like prophets among an erring flock, a cross between Job and Jehovah. Of all the variegated Afrikaner totems, I think the most pertinent is a pocket knife which lies preserved inside this little house. With this implement Kruger once amputated his own thumb after a hunting accident. He chopped the thumb off cleanly enough, and his women folk sprinkled sugar on it, as an antiseptic, but the gangrene set in after all. So they killed a goat and extracted its stomach and told Kruger to plunge his hand into the steaming entrails. 'This old Boer remedy succeeded,' said the President proudly: and of all his many tales of reminiscence none is more vividly expressive of the Afrikaner tradition, a *mélange* of hardships, rebuffs, gangrenous attacks, brave women, huntsmen, knives, stoical courage and old Boer remedies. The soul of a people is crystallized in that old pocket knife, preserved among the presidential trophies.

Such small symbolisms, however, do not satisfy the demands of fervid nationalism: and since this is the capital of Afrikaner chauvinism, there stands on a neighbouring hill a monumental talisman of patriotic pride. The *hegira* of the Boers, from which they date their redemption and their nationhood, was the Great Trek of 1836. With their wives and their animals, their poke bonnets and their ox-wagons, they migrated from the coastal districts to these remote regions of the interior, where they could live in peace and treat their black men as they pleased, free from the restraints of the British. Quibblers sometimes suspect the motives of the movement; Englishmen sometimes point out that innumerable British adventurers had done the trip before; but the ox-wagons of the Voortrek are as vivid and significant to the Afrikaner as is the *Mayflower* to the matrons of the English-

Speaking Union. To mark the centenary of the trek, they erected upon a dominating hilltop an enormous, bulbous, arrogant blockhouse of a monument, a sentinel above the city. Its architural ancestry is confused. Some say it is based upon the mausoleum of Halicarnassus in Asia Minor. Others claim it has Bantu affiliations, and reflections of the mysterious Zimbabwe civilization that flourished to the north. Some of the sculpture is Italian. But nothing could be more Afrikaner than the laager of stone ox-wagons which surrounds the building, and indeed, if you half-close your eyes and let your fancy play, you will discover that the monument *en masse* bears a distinct if swollen resemblance to Kruger himself.

Inside it is vast and echoing, and decorated with reliefs illustrating the advance of European civilization into these dark parts—invigorating battle scenes, in which countless screaming black savages are being trampled underfoot or disintegrated with gunfire, and homely pastoral gatherings, in which the black man stands in grateful subservience behind his Boer master. (One such panel, says the guide-book convincingly, is 'the only existing portrayal of a battle between men on horseback and men riding oxen'. The Matabele rode to war on battle-oxen, with viciously sharpened horns). In the basement there is a sacramental ox-wagon, and a perpetual flame, and a symbolic tomb. 'Who's in there?' I asked an African cleaner who was dusting the steps of this sarcophagus (other black men are only admitted on Tuesday afternoons). 'Search me, Baas,' he replied with a grin, 'but he's been here a *long* time, I know that. Eeeh, Baas, a *very* long time!' Once a year, by a Pyramidical or Druidic arrangement, a shaft of sunshine appears through a vent in the high roof and falls upon an inscription on the tomb: 'Ons vir Jou, Suid-Afrika', runs this sunlit oath—'We for Thee, South Africa!'

All this is taken very seriously by the Afrikaners, who find it easy to combine a kind of glazed ancestor-worship with the austerities of their Calvinist creed; and every year several thousand of them grow black bushy beards or dress up in bonnets and aprons to assemble on this hill-side, pour a meta-

physical libation, remember the ox-wagons, and pledge themselves to eternal Afrikanerdom. In Pretoria to-day their nationalism stands triumphant. Here the old feud between Boer and
Briton is still fought, and when a Pretoria Afrikaner says he stands
for an Afrikaner Republic, and to blazes with all the fiddle-de-
dee of Crown and Commonwealth—when he makes some such
bold statement of principle he is envisaging, as often as not,
a return to the old patriarchal Boer state, governed exclusively
by the old Boer values. In this city you can sense all too clearly
the niggling inferiority complex that animates so much of the
Afrikaner's political thinking, and which stems partly from the
years when the British lorded it in Church Square, and did their
best to eliminate the heritage of the Voortrekkers. Many Afrikaners freely admit the influence of this complex. In Pretoria I
met one young Afrikaner intellectual of striking presence and
ability. He was a Rhodes scholar, graced with remarkable good
looks and fluency of expression, and of an old and distinguished
Boer family: but from time to time, as we talked over the dinner
table, there crept into his conversation an oddly incongruous
note of petulant defiance. With a slight blush or a toss of his
head, he would suddenly blurt out some clumsy anglophobic
anecdote, or make a cruel jibe at the Queen, or remind me unnecessarily (rather like an Arab refugee bewailing lost munificence) how harshly his family had been impoverished by the
Boer War—before subsiding again, after an awkward moment
of silence, into his usual urbanity and *politesse*. After dinner he
took me aside and apologized. 'You must understand', he said
a little shyly, 'that we Afrikaners are a people with a chip on our
shoulder—bear with us, my friend, if you can. We shall grow
out of it!'

There is an obvious connection between this insidious intro-
spection and the Afrikaner theories of racial hierarchy. Some
say the Boer War was the true progenitor of apartheid, and that
the Afrikaner is haunted by the fear that Briton and African
will one day coalesce against the Volk. Just as the Jews sometimes revenge their persecutions upon their Arab neighbours, so
the Boers sublimate their anti-British grievances in the principle

of white supremacy. But the desire to be masters of white South Africa, not to speak of black, is still almost an obsession among thousands of Afrikaners. Indeed, there is a distinct streak of paranoia to this national aspiration, and you will hear so much about the iniquities of Lords Roberts and Milner, and be told so repeatedly about living on mushrooms in British concentration camps, and be instructed so horrifically in British atrocities, and be so wearied with eulogies of the old Boer ways, that before long you may feel one more fungus, just one more atrocity, a single supplementary ox-wagon will make you scream. It is rather as though every Welshman in Cardiff were suddenly to be inspired by the dottiest ambitions of Welsh nationalism (and indeed, the two peoples have much in common). The Broederbond, the secret society of Afrikaner nationalism, is the supreme example of these morbid tendencies: nobody knows who its members are, and if you ask an Afrikaner notable whether he is a Broeder, he will look unconvincingly blank, or deny it, or evade the issue in a paroxysm of coughing, or reply blandly: 'Yes, my dear chap, I am, but of course it's purely a cultural organization, dedicated to the advancement of our folk culture —rather like the British Council, you know, did you happen to read their admirable pamphlet on basket-making in east Norfolk?' There seems to me something excessively silly about the Broederbond, with its secret rituals and tests of moral purity: but it is sometimes rather creepy to stumble upon its traces as you wander about South Africa, and hear the hooded tone of voice in which people talk about it.

To-day the Afrikaner is politically supreme in South Africa, and during my winter there the Nationalist Party was all-powerful. Afrikaans has not only replaced English as the predominant language, but has actually succeeded in producing a respectable literature of its own—this in a vernacular that was, only fifty years ago, no more than a kind of kitchen Dutch. The Pretoria air is thick with the homely phrases of Afrikaans ('No Oop' means 'Now Open', 'Foei tog!' is 'What a pity!', and the extreme zealots of the city, revelling in their ascendancy, will sometimes refuse to talk to you in English. 'Would you mind speaking English?' I asked one such enthusiast on the telephone. '*You* speak English if you like,' he said, 'but I prefer to answer in Afrikaans.' The old symbols of English supremacy are being whittled away, little by little (the South African sailor, stripped of his bell-bottoms, is now an exotic animal indeed). The administration and the Civil Service is heavily Afrikaner. There are great corporations founded upon Afrikaner capital, and even in the high-vaulted chambers of the mining companies, once exclusively Anglo-Jewish, you may find Afrikaners sitting comfortably in high places. When I was in South Africa, indeed, there was an Afrikaner bid to gain control of the 'Corner House', one of the greatest of these mining concerns; and it was extraordinary how avidly the Volk watched the proceedings, with the eager eye of nationalism, and queer to find some shaggy platteland farmer, ankle-deep in potatoes, remarking upon the course of so esoteric a struggle. The patriotism of the Afrikaner is resolute, ingrained, parochial and almost unanimous, and a triumph for one is a triumph for all.

But now that Afrikanerdom rules South Africa, stronger than the British both in numbers and in influence, perhaps the arrogance of these emotions will abate. There is much less need for secret societies, now that an Afrikaner Government declares the Union's policies, and far less reason for atavistic impulses. Perhaps the Volkswil, the supreme court of Afrikaner ambition, may lose some of its chauvinistic overtones, and the Boer learn at last to live in calm friendship with his neighbours. But I doubt it. There is a nagging sense of doom and fatalism to this patriotic mystique, a hint of the incurably melancholic. Some shadowy intuition tells me that for all its determination and talent and success Afrikanerdom is not destined for serenity, and that Pretoria will never recapture those blithe patriarchial days of the old republic, when Kruger's rocking-chair creaked reassuringly on its veranda, and the burghers said amen.

5

COUNTRY LIVING

That brave old republic was a pastoral state, firmly embedded in the land, and the Afrikaner is still at heart an agrarian. Sometimes a buried migratory instinct, a muffled bugle-call, urges him over the next horizon, to places where (as he likes to put it in his romantic moments) he cannot see the smoke from his neighbour's chimney; but he is at his most characteristic in his settled country condition, among his ox-teams and his Bantu. In the layered society of the South African countryside you may taste his prejudices in the raw, and sample some of his earthier ideas about divine intentions and the hierarchies of race.

Some of the richest and most indulgent of Afrikaner farms lie in the luscious citrus country to the north of Johannesburg, where the grim plateau softens into hillocks, and the valleys are fresh with orange groves. On the edge of the road, as you drive past, black and white urchins sit beside piles of fruit, spitting their pips into the ditch and trying half-heartedly to engage your custom. Vivacious clusters of Afrikan women, dazzling in blues and yellows, squat gesticulating among their bags and bundles, waiting for buses. There are pleasant reclining farm-houses, white and prosperous; and here and there you pass a guest ranch or a 'resort', with a swimming pool and self-satisfied girls on horses and, as the brochures idly say, 'an excellent licensed airstrip'. Sometimes a polished buggy clops down a lane, driven by an elderly woman in black, with a piccaninny boy straight-backed and silent on the seat beside her: but more often it is a big American car that comes sweeping by, at the wheel a woman with rhinestones on the corners of her spectacles, in the back seat a solitary black labourer, like a subservient St. Bernard. This is a well-heeled countryside, comfortably domesticated. Most of the game has gone, and only the tawny dust, the space, and the black people remain to convince you that you are in Africa.

A few small towns co-ordinate the life of such a neighbourhood, and lie basking among the citrus groves with a seductive languor. Their streets are wide and their pace is leisurely, and the bank building is usually new and grand. Beside the main square stands the town's hotel, with a veranda and clumps of gloomy plants in tubs, a rambling, insidiously peeling structure of homely affiliations. They do not serve alcohol until six o'clock, and the waiter has often gone next door for a chat with the barber; but be careful: cosy though they may feel, and easygoing, it is one of the peculiarities of these hostelries that reveille is at crack of dawn, with a sickly cup of tea and a brusque and business-like good morning. Like the Middle West, the Transvaal is proud of its diligence and labour, and does not pander to sleepy-heads. In the hall of the hotel there hangs an ornate certificate, certifying membership of the Association of Rand Pioneers and Women Pioneers ('They Did Their Level Best'), and an old photograph of a tumble-down stage coach being ferried across a river, its crew confronting the camera, apparently infuriated by its intrusion, with their arms akimbo and their moustaches ferociously acock. A smell of cigar smoke and over-cooking pervades such an inn as this, giving it a thick avuncular bouquet, and whenever you look into the smoking-room, morning or night, the same couple of middle-aged Afrikaner farmers seem to be leaning on their elbows and talking about money.

A big Dutch Reformed Church, of modern but complacent design, stands in the middle of the square. Both its clocks have stopped, in common with nearly every other public clock in the Union: but for the rest it seems to be bursting with energy, activity and success. A gilded weathercock stands proudly on its tower, its lawns are carefully tended, its notice-board is trim and prosperous, and in the evening, when the choir assembles to practise and the predikant presides over a conference of penitents, neon lights shine brazenly through its windows. Around the corner is the shopping street: dowdy drapers, windows of insecticide and tractor spares, a well-stocked bookshop, the local newspaper, a juke-box in a coffee shop, a turbanned Indian merchant staring at you gravely over a mountain of junky suitcases. Along these arcades whirl the black people, the men shambling or loping, the women gossiping squeakily, and the adorable children all eyes and impudence, with smiles of response as swift and enchanting as the flash of a swallow. Here and there a white farmer steps from his car and walks aloofly through this shifting crowd into the chemist's, and in the coffee shop the white youths in their loud shirts and the skinny girls in their petticoats and pony-tails drink fizzy lemonade through straws and read about the film stars.

This is the centre of town, dominated by bank, church, hotel and farmers' money. As you walk away from the square, though, you will find the character of the place changing. The buildings thin out, and lose their stolidity, and the roads degenerate from tarmac to dirt and then to rutted tracks, and the big cars do not stop, but speed by with an irritated blast of horns. You leave the houses of the white burghers, sunning themselves on their stoeps, and find yourself among the second-class citizens. Here is the Indian quarter, where the slim young girls wear saris and ribbons in their hair, and play about in the street with a curious air of elegant lassitude: there is a mosque with a crescent moon above it, and the houses are infused with calm, and cupidity, and the suggestion of incense. And here, by way of contrast, are the sleazy homes of the Africans. Their location is tucked away among the scrubby trees on the outskirts of the town, and seems in a perpetual state of pyrotechnics. Boys ride dizzily about on bicycles, a laugh passes raucously from house to house, on the football field three or four referees try to maintain some state of order by a hopeless *obbligato* of whistles. A few prim little girls play netball. Ugly old men smoke cob pipes. Battalions of villainous youths, coarse and froward, disconcert you by replying to your nervous greeting with smiles of ineffable sweetness and innocence. The location is ablaze with life, fun, squalor and incompetence.

Nothing could illustrate more effectively the meaning of apartheid than the gulf that divides these separate communities, and emphasizes so vividly the disparities between their cultures. You may think those Africans look contented enough, and indeed they do: but in the minds of many of their white neighbours they are little better than animals, and scarcely more entitled to privileges or blessings than a well-disposed ox or a cart-horse. Beneath the surface of the Afrikaner countryside, even in such gentle orange-blossom regions, there lies a dark stratum of repression. Outside many a small rural town, among the little empires of the farmers, you will often see a line of black men working silently in the fields, dressed in sacks, and sometimes encouraged by a white overseer with a whip, riding a horse. These are convicts, hired out for an infinitesimal wage. Some have perhaps been convicted of leaving their passes at home, or breaking a curfew; others, arrested in the street, have deliberately chosen to work on a prison farm, rather than face a trial. They provide, in short, a kind of legalized slave labour, often condemned to work in servitude for acts or omissions that are not, by any reasonable standards of morality or democratic law, offences at all. Sometimes they are housed by the farmers themselves, in private prisons at the bottom of farmyards. Elsewhere the farmers sometimes club together, like devoted charitable workers, to build a communal prison. 'It's really a very convenient prison,' a farmer remarked to me, pointing out one such jail, 'and it won't take us more than a year to get all our money back.'

Sometimes stories of atrocious physical cruelties emerge from these captivities, and often enough a visit to an Afrikaner farm will leave you with a haunting vision of a living serf system, a survival from an abandoned past, like a coelocanth or a heraldic ritual. The farmer will certainly greet you with genuine and heart-warming hospitality, stumbling through his welcome in his stilted English, with his hat courteously in his hand and his thumb hastily adjusting the straps of his braces. In a trice there will be coffee (you can see his bosomy black cook protruding slightly from behind the refrigerators in the kitchen) and probably some fruit or biscuits. His wife will hover attentively around you for a moment or two, before gliding away to her knitting, and sometimes a white foreman looks in with an inquiry or a broken fan-belt. The farmhouse is furnished with austere taste. President Kruger may well glare down at you through his whiskers from the dining-room wall. There is a portrait of a leathery old grandmother above the mantelpiece. Everything is kindly, and honest, and frank.

But watch that farmer when, a few moments later, he takes you out among his Africans in the yard. A strange change then overcomes his personality, and his whole being becomes suddenly harsh and domineering. This is partly because he is talking to simple black men, and partly because he has been educated since childhood to think of them as inferiors, and partly because they are probably lazy and shiftless, and partly because (for all his generosity) he is damned if he is going to alter his tone of voice just because a visiting Englishman is present: but it is partly, you cannot help suspecting, because a streak of sadism and a nugget of fear charges his attitudes towards every African. The black man has always been either his enemy or his slave, and the motion of the times has not yet adjusted these inherited sentiments. The farmhands stand there in their raggety clothes, floppy hats on their heads and trousers subsiding hangdog over their feet, and the farmer clasps his thick stick, and raps out his orders, and indicates the different labourers as he might poke a sack of potatoes; and you can feel that farmyard heavy with the tensions and resentments and forebodings that have, through all the centuries, burdened the relationship between lord and helot.

Sometimes, as in the Johannesburg locations, an uncanny sense of predestination infuses this society. The Kruger National Park, in the north-eastern Transvaal, is managed according to the precepts of the Balance of Nature: no animal is artificially protected, and the survival of the fittest is the rule among both beasts and park administrators. Similar concepts govern the

affairs of the Afrikaner countryside. At the back of many a farmer's mind is the conviction that God Himself has decreed the stratification of the races, and that man (whatever his inclinations) is powerless to oppose it. The white man must be, by sacred ordinance, master over the black; and the African is condemned for ever and ever, by the authority of Holy Writ, to be a hewer of wood and a drawer of water. I remember one Transvaal farmer, a young man with a deep voice and gently protruding teeth, who remarked to me as we stood beside his thresher: 'What you foreigners don't understand is that we *can't* change things, even if we wanted to. These people here'—and he pointed to his black labourers, sweating at their work around us—'these people have always been like this, don't you see, and you can't alter them just by passing a law or *wishing*.' To such a man there is an organic truth to the shape of South African society. He thinks as an aristocrat might have thought, before the burning of the Bastille, or a geographer before Columbus, or a conservative Astronomer Royal before the advent of the satellites and the space rockets. He cannot grasp the peculiar heresies of the outsider: and if you venture to breathe a diffident word about racial progress and the advance of the black man, why, he will give you another cup of coffee, he will slap you jovially on the back, but he will think you a Galileo, a Copernicus, a James Watt, a rocketeer, subject to dotty visions and wild theories, or delusions about the solar system.

I once called upon a predikant of the Dutch Reformed Church in a very small Transvaal village. His church was new and luxurious, his house polished and french-windowed, and in his garden there stood a brand-new German car. He reminded me of those bright gregarious low-church parsons so often to be found in well-meant unction among the communities of the American East. He was young and slightly gushing, sat on the edge of his study table and swung his legs rhythmically, and was distinguished by a certain glossy intelligence. His village, though, was poor and shabby, with a couple of stores and a butcher's shop, a police station with a blue lamp and the Union flag, and an old African tailor working away at a treadle machine on the porch of a wooden house. This was a completely Afrikaner society, and the predikant told me that only twice before, in all his ten years there, had he had occasion to speak English. 'I'm studying the language intensively, though,' he added, jumping from his table and going to his desk: and sure enough he was laboriously translating a government pamphlet on racial policy, and had underlined in red pencil the phrase 'biological assimilation' as needing further linguistic clarification. What did it mean, exactly? he asked me: but alas, I could not help him. 'Anyway,' he said kindly, 'one day Afrikaans must be the only language in South Africa. I am studying English only for convenience. It must happen. We do not want to oppress our friends the British, but one day this must inevitably become a unilingual state.'

Yes, said this clergyman breezily, swinging his legs again, history is, after all, God-ordained; and so is race. 'God divided us into our races, and we must respect his divisions. No, my friend, I would not shake hands with any black man—not anywhere—in no circumstances—but I do believe, now, and I believe this very firmly, that you must always treat the natives fairly. I always tell my people, you must never withhold any money, not a tickey, from your servants' pay. You must treat them fairly in every respect. I always tell my people, I tell them, your natives are human beings, and you mustn't cheat them.' You must be just as fair (he added, with a look of triumphant piety) 'as you would be with a European.'

And what would happen, said I, if an African walked into one of his services, in the grand church next door? 'I would have him removed. That church is for Europeans, and it would be wrong to allow a native to worship there. God divided the races for His own purposes, and it is not for us to doubt His wisdom.'

'Or if a Chinaman turned up one day, or an Eskimo?'

'No, my church is not for Asiatics. I would send them away. But now you must not misunderstand me,' he added earnestly. tapping his knee with his forefinger. 'I don't say they shouldn't have a service at all. If there was no other church for them to attend I would hold a service myself, not inside my church, of course, but in a field if necessary. I feel this very strongly: that no man, whatever his colour, whatever his race, wheresoever he cometh from, should be deprived of the opportunity of worshipping Him who is the creator of us all.'

I had no adequate response to this unimpeachable sentiment, and so our interview ended: but as I left the house the predikant grasped my arm, rather in the Rotarian manner, and pointed across the street outside. An elderly black woman, dressed in voluminous coarse draperies, was hobbling out of a shop, screaming something in a searing treble over her shoulder. She walked to the gutter, withdrew a hand from some hideous recess of her clothing, closed one nostril and emptied her nose noisily into the street. Then, wiping her face with her skirts, she turned around, still screeching, and disappeared creakily indoors. 'You see?' said the predikant, in his most telling observation of the afternoon. 'My dear friend, we are not unkindly, but you must live among them to understand the Truth!'

These are extremes. They illustrate one level of thought, perhaps the most pervasive, among the Afrikaner plattelander. But they ignore many a worthy old-fashioned burgher whose dealings with his black men are kindly and paternal, and who has established with them the same warm and protective relationship that often dignified the slave plantations of the American South. There are many Afrikaner countrymen whose belief in apartheid is not curdled by any taste for brutality, or sanctified by any obscure Biblical allusions. More important, there are (I believe) a growing number of rural Afrikaners who cannot whole-heartedly subscribe to these racial conceptions at all, who realize that one day the black man must be given a fair chance, and who are by slow degrees, with infinite caution and psychological effort, accustoming themselves to the notion that this is a changing world. I sympathize with the Afrikaner Abrahams, upright among the flocks and heather; and I am sorry for the dogmatists, with their several infallible justifications for serfdom; but I believe this anachronistic society is doomed, and I admire most those country Afrikaners who have the courage to desert its traditions.

6

MINES

Perhaps three million Africans have adapted themselves to this rural régime, and live among the white people as labourers or smallholders. Three million more have become city men in the locations. But there are also, at any one time, another 300,000 black men working in the gold mines of the Reef, the prime source of South Africa's power. Anywhere from Springs to Randfontein, if you stand still and try hard enough, you may fancy you hear the shaking of the rock drills beneath your feet; and every minute of every day of the year the great mines are working, and the ore is being processed, and the dust extracted, and the gleaming gold bars shipped away to London and eventually America, where they are promptly buried again beneath the ground at Fort Knox. This queer process colours the life of Transvaal and the Union, and gives it an Orwellian tinge: for to my mind there is something intrinsically chill about gold, an unkindly metal, and something false and creepy about its perverse importance to the world.

There is a suggestion of 1984, too, to the system by which the mine companies secure their black labour. All over southern Africa, north to Nyasaland and Tanganyika, west to Angola, east to Mozambique, hundreds of thousands of Africans look to the mines of the Rand for their bride-money, their adventure and their self-esteem. The tribal wars have gone, leaving only a sad residue of battle-dances, feuds and ritual murders, and to many a young tribesman a year in the mines is a test of honour and a proof of manhood. This fortunate tradition is naturally exploited by the mine companies, whose magazines are full of suitable folk-lore: 'He is gone, he is gone,' the Pondoland maidens allegedly croon in their kraals, 'my brave lover has gone to Goli! How I wish he may return to me, his manhood proved in the bowels of the earth, rich and handsome, my warrior home from war!' Innumerable recruiting offices, slapped across the face of a continent, enable the young warrior to fulfil these aspirations. Each is emblazoned with an enticing four-quartered heraldic shield—in one corner a Pondo maiden waves farewell to the Johannesburg train, in another her lover returns triumphant to his kraal—and each is known as Kwa Teba, after an early recruiting official named Taberer. Over a large proportion of southern Africa, Kwa Teba is as familiar as the sunrise; and through several generations the young men have volunteered in their endless stream, to be packed off to the Reef by train, truck, boat or aeroplane. Tucking their blankets firmly around them, grasping their knobbly sticks, they march off wondering into the great unknown of the Rand. Sometimes you may see them walking in anxious crocodile through the streets of Johannesburg, open-mouthed and crinkle-browed: and I was once visiting a gold mine at the very moment when a group of such innocents arrived from Basutoland for the first time. They had never left their kraals before, and everything was strange to them. It was a whiplash rainy day, and those poor Africans were buried in gaudy blankets and burdened with bags and boxes, packages tied up with old rope, paper bags, muffled bundles and socks. They stumbled down from the truck for all the world like lost wet souls arriving in purgatory, or orphans at a Dickensian institution; and they wandered across the road to their compound, trailing string, drapery and bewilderment, gazing about them vacantly and drenched in rain.

Their transition is probably no stranger, in fact, than the experience of some rock-bottom Tennessee hill-billy committed to the United States Army, or even of the little Welsh housemaids of my childhood who used to arrive direct from the Carmarthenshire valleys to pilfer the silver and impregnate the second floor with sixpenny face powder. The black mine recruits are sorted, and inspected, and tested, and weighed, and put into barracks just as soldiers are: and some of the more progressive mines even give them vocational tests, and make them fit pieces of wood together in a pattern, or construct a bridge out of two old planks and a beer barrel. The compounds in which they live often bear a hazy metaphysical resemblance to the old cavalry lines at Aldershot, and the white men who look after them do so with a kind of welfare officer *bonhomie*, and sometimes talk about 'my chaps' in an authentic subaltern's croak.

Still, you cannot escape the eeriness of the big mine compounds, so notorious of legend, in which these thousands of Africans, straight from the mud huts and the reserves, are fattened and fed and fostered for the business of the mines. In some places a ramp leads from the compound to the shaft of the mine itself, and the men shuffle directly from their dormitories to the hoist; and by the nature of things there is a sense of inhumanity to the process, an insinuation of cattle-fodder or salt mines. 'We do what we can,' one good compound manager told me as we inspected his arrangements, 'but let's face it, there's something evil about the system, and you can't abolish an evil with an extra pound of sugar.' The mineworker, willy-nilly, leads an unwholesome kind of life. There are no women in these compounds, and few of the homely hugger-mugger comforts of African life, and no children, and no animals (except that, in the humaner compounds, you may find a couple of smart baboons tied to a stake in the yard, or a small grey antelope ruminating outside the kitchen). Life feels subtly and unpleasantly artificial. Kaffir beer, the only alcohol legally allowed to Africans in the Union, simmers and bubbles in huge metal vats; and when the miners queue for their dinner, in their sweaty shirts and helmets, the cooks bang on the side of their tureens with big tin spoons, and ladle out the food (rich and plentiful) rather as you might throw a haunch to some compliant carnivore. I was not shocked by the mine compounds, which are not by any means cruel places, and which do allow the African to preserve his old loyalties: but I found them disagreeably haunting, like the memory of a bad dream at lunchtime.

All over the Rand they stand, square buildings with gardens or yards in the centre, and from the passing road they do look

MINES

misleadingly like prisons, so blank and faceless are their exterior walls. On a Sunday morning, though, the mineworkers spill out of their gates and into the sunshine, collecting their passes as they go: and all along the Reef, in grey mining towns and down tree-shaded suburban avenues, the black miners stroll and gossip, wrapped in the blankets of their reservations (pink and blue and vivid) or plastered in brilliantine. And when the sun sets you may see the stragglers sauntering by with their hands in their pockets, plucking at a guitar or sucking tediously at a mouth-organ, before the curfew falls and they must scuttle like schoolboys back to their quarters. It is, of course, the policy of the mine companies to keep them as 'tribal' as possible, to avoid contamination with those slick, wide-shouldered urbanites who joke the bitter hours away in Orlando and Meadowlands. 'These are honest tribal Kaffirs,' the mine overseer will tell you, 'none of your detribalized scum: I have plenty of time for these boys, before they start thinking they're as clever as you.'

Each Sunday morning, in the pursuance of this policy, there is a mine dance at one of the Reef compounds, when the black miners from a dozen different tribes perform their ancestral dances before an audience of delighted black colleagues and white tourists with Leicas. These are unforgettable spectacles. An electric air of force and virility exudes from the dancers as they sweep, team by team, into the arena in their bright feathers and their leopard skins. Their shields, to be sure, are made of cardboard, and their masks sometimes fall off, and their instruments are devised of old petrol tins or bits of iron ('equipment is provided with the help of the management', we are told piously by the company, which makes a profit of several million pounds each year); but even these symptoms of pathos or sham are swamped by the animal vigour of it all. An extraordinary percussive instrument, like a gigantic home-made xylophone, is set up beside the arena: and while the dancers contort themselves upon the gravel, and the singers bay and the drummers drum phrenetically, four or five men beat out an endless repetitive tune upon its keys, with a violent vibratory descant from the tins, drums and wire contraptions that form its sound-

59

box. Sometimes, in the frenzy, an African leaps from the audience and dances all by himself in the corner of the arena, wiggling his hips and rolling his great white eyes: and sometimes a clown among the performers suddenly jumps to the edge of the spectators and squats like a big funny animal beside the front row, making faces, until a little white girl in a frilly pink frock, wondering for a moment or two whether to laugh or scream, decides at last to find it amusing and giggles helplessly into her ruched nylon.

The dances vary greatly. The Basutos, huddled mournfully in their blankets and shaded in battered trilby hats, crouch together like down-and-outs and sing in a depressing kind of plain-song. The Zulus perform an anaemic version of the horrific war dance, all feathers and furious faces, which used to strike a chill into the hearts of their listening enemies. A man from Swaziland, magnificent of physique, contemptuous of bearing, sings a glorious song of triumph to a background of horns and thudding drums. A team from Mozambique, the most overwhelmingly vigorous of all, prances with such marvellous abandon, plays its music with such wild anarchy, excites the entire arena so irresistibly that its performance ends in a cacophony of whistles and drums and xylophones and laughter and shouts and the clatter of shields; and when at last the dancers leave the arena with long loping strides, two or three inflamed spectators are left jigging aimlessly behind, like headless chickens running around a farmyard.

Finally there are the shuffle-dancers. About the beginning of this century the people of the Baca tribe, in Natal, were taught by a progressive Christian evangelist to perform a kind of step dance, coupled with rhythmic clappings and slapping of hips. When some of these people went to work in the docks at Durban, they found that the Wellington boots issued to dockers were an admirable adjunct to such comical displays: and so they evolved the gum-boot dance, one of the South African phenomena. On they come, dressed identically in shirts and white gloves and jeans and gum-boots, while two men crouch solemnly over mandolines and play a lugubrious metallic melody. The dance begins sedately enough, a sort of heavy-footed tap dance: but every now and then, without warning, the dancers are abruptly seized with a paroxysm of violent energy; and all at once their hands beat out a riotous unison rhythm on their gum-boots, with indescribable speed and precision—*slappity-:.a* - *slap, slappity-slappity-slap*—before subsiding again, like a reviving epileptic, into their ponderous evangelical routine. So dead-pan is the performance, and so unpredictable are these moments of hilarious boot-slapping, that the audience sits poised in a state of breathless expectancy: and the Africans in the audience, tensed in an ecstasy of impatience, explode with pleasure when the paroxysms occur, and shake the roof of the arena with their laughter. The black African is a melancholy figure, in the context of the times; but if you think he is in a state of permanent depression or discontent, watch his gleaming eyes when the gum-boot dancers shuffle on.

Outside in a small shed four or five white women prepare the tea, for there is an interval in the mine dance, and the white visitors with their cameras crowd outside and eat a sweet biscuit in the sunshine. As you stand there talking, or admiring each other's hats, you can hear the distant insistent sounds of drums and chanting; here in the tea shed you are lapped in gentility, but always around the corner there is Africa. The South African mines are heavily segregated, and the industrial colour bar is both potent and debilitating. The black miners are well-fed and well-housed, and often cared for with genuine affection: but there is no hope whatsoever, not a glimmering of a chance, not the faintest possibility of an African becoming anything more than a boss-boy in the mines, however able or courageous or hard-working. Life underground, as on the surface, is rigidly stratified: here shale, here reef; here damp, here dry; here exclusively white, there irrevocably black. When you go down the hoist with the white mine superviser, you will see how the racial feudalism of South Africa extends even to the face of the reef. A black man brings you your boots and your helmet and your overalls, as you prepare yourself in the changing-room; and a black man hands you your face-rag as you enter the hoist; and a black man blows his whistle and drives you in his trollies along the underground corridor; and a black man helps you off with your jacket when, as you approach the stope, the heat suddenly blasts you like a sirocco. And there at the very war-front of the mine, where the big rock chamber is lit only by helmet-lamps, and there is a deafening clatter of drills, and a smell of dust and sweat and black skin—there is your Basuto blanket-boy, his guitar and his bundles discarded, stripped for action at his battle station. An Afrikaner overseer crouches behind him, and grins a welcome to you as you slither down the rubble; but flat on his back in an alcove of the rock is the African driller, helmeted and swathed in sweat. He pauses in his work as you approach, but the supervisor gives him a flicker of his torch, and he is off again, smiling broadly through his dirt. He holds his big drill with his feet, and he lies there like some hefty freak or prodigy, a hand-less painter or a three-legged man, his whole body shaking with the vibration of the drill, and the very air about him shuddering with its noise. This is why he went to Kwa Teba, in the shambled trading store of his distant kraal; and this is why they stuff him with fish and Irish stew, and tie a gangling baboon to a stake, a mile above our heads in the compound.

The gold mines are the staples of South African wealth, run by companies of admirable urbanity. Some of the gold magnates are men of liberal (or at least perceptive) vision, and would like to see a settled labour force, with its wives and children and household goods, gradually replacing the migratory system and the compounds. But the Afrikaner zealots prefer things as they are, for this is apartheid *in excelsis*. The African leaves his mud huts voluntarily; works for the white man without joining the white man's community; is sheltered from all political activities and ambitions; is treated with aloof but often paternal care; and is finally shipped back to his village again, theoretically to resume, as good black men should, the taboos and rituals of his tribal heritage. Nobody ill-treats him. He need not come if he does not want to. He usually goes home, as the mining companies like to say, four or five pounds heavier than when he arrived,

MINES

This is a blinkered looking-glass outlook, for the system cannot last. Mines or no mines, gold or no gold, the black African is slowly discarding his indigenous ways and moving into the world of the white man. I do not like the synthesis of cultures that is, for the moment, the product of this process, the vacuum that underlies the Johannesburg locations, the hollowness and insecurity of it all; but I believe it to be, alas, one of the profound truths of the twentieth century. The raw urban locations, not the sheltering compounds, represent the future of the African (and therefore, by a natural syllogism, the future of the Afrikaner, too). Still, these are early years, and the compounds have many long decades ahead of them, and many a hundred thousand more Africans to undergo their vocational tests. At every moment of every day a stream of excited or apprehensive black people is pouring towards the Transvaal, trudging through the reserves of Zululand or the Transkei, hitch-hiking through Mozambique, punted in rafts across the Zambesi, crammed aboard the train from Basutoland, or sitting in rigid astonishment aboard the eight Dakotas by which the mine companies fly in labourers from the north. Without this flood of black manpower, pouring ceaselessly into the compounds, South Africa would be bankrupt in the twinkling of a speculator's bloodshot eye.

7

CENTRE CITY

The political capital of Afrikanerdom is Pretoria, the city of the Voortrekkers, where we may assume the be-robed high stewards of the Broederbond to sit in veiled cabal. The most thoroughly Afrikaner province of the Union, though, is the Orange Free State, the second of the old Boer republics. It lies to the south-west of the Transvaal, inhabited by about a million people, three-quarters of them black, and by and large it is a harsh, open, scrubby country, a place of endless rolling veldt, of cattlemen and ranchers. When you steam through these spreading plains in the air-conditioned Blue Train, you can all but see the Boer commandos sweeping towards the Cape in their raggle-taggle troops, or imagine the trekkers ringed in the security of their laagers; and indeed, so deep has the ox-wagon mystique of the Great Trek bitten into the soul of the Afrikaner that some people believe the whole public psychology of the Orange Free State to be dominated by the concept of the circle, inherited from those protective encampments. Certainly the people of Bloemfontein are fond of saying that theirs is the 'centre city', from which circles of influence and activity radiate mysteriously to coast and hinterland; and once you start thinking about circles you will notice such mystic symbols wherever you look, and detect (like a persecuted paranoiac) the circular complex concealed in every harmless conversation.

Bloemfontein is the judicial capital of the Union, and a stronghold of the Reformed Church. It is not a gay city. It lies sprawling in the plain, wide, pale and spacious, guarded by the dome of an observatory (the atmosphere is crystal) and dominated by the earnest structures of the law courts—panelled throughout, as

64

the publicists like to say, in one of the less fortunate national symbols, stink-wood. The flavour of Bloemfontein is heavily austere. Beside your bed at the hotel you will find the Bible in Afrikaans, printed by the Cambridge University Press, and when I was there the authorites had just decided that public dancing on a Sunday was, as they had long suspected, wicked, and must therefore be prohibited. It goes without saying that you may not fish on Sundays, and Sunday trains may only run in the Orange Free State if they have begun their journeys outside the province. As everywhere in the Union, women are not allowed in the bars of Bloemfontein: and it is depressing indeed to peer through the curtained doorways of these unhappy saloons for a glimpse of their brandy-stained smoky squalor, the ultimate antithesis of jollity. All these devout regulations are firmly enforced, and the Dutch Church community of Bloemfontein has produced, in its time, some virile Christians. One moderator, finding an irrespectful pedestrian obstructing the progress of his car, took out a shotgun and fired at him: and when, by some inexplicable divine intervention, the tower of his church fell down, this same churchman announced from his pulpit that it would on no account be rebuilt until the Union of South Africa was declared a republic. I telephoned one distinguished clergyman to ask for an interview. 'No, no,' he replied testily, with a distinctly papal turn of phrase, 'we have no time for audiences, we have our Pentecostal services to prepare.' I asked another cleric if he thought Catholic immigration a healthy thing for South Africa. 'I can't say I do,' he said seriously, touching the tips of his fingers and looking at me over his spectacles, 'because you see we are a *Christian* country.' When I stepped off my train in this dour city I asked my taxi-driver if he was an Afrikaner. 'We are all Afrikaners in this country now,' he replied, without turning his head. 'We only vary according to the degree of our integration with God. Now, where d'you want to go?'

But this flourishing religion, though strait-laced (especially among the extreme 'Dopper' sects), also has dignity. I went to a Sunday morning service in Bloemfontein, and found it both compelling and attractive. As I walked up the steps into the white-painted church, two or three deacons hurried past me, smelling faintly of soap and mothballs. They were clean-shaven young men of sprightly bearing, wearing black frock-coats and wing collars, and they hastened into the church like polished black beetles, their shards pressed and burnished. Inside, the congregation was no less meticulously prepared; the women in clothes of unexpected brightness, the men sombre but prosperous, and only one small child in sight, dressed in virginal modesty. The Afrikaner is not a man of half-measures, and this was a whole-hog service, during which not a wandering fancy strayed into the beguiling sunshine outside, not an eye roved along the neighbouring pews, not a single beflowered hat was tilted in coquetry. The predikant was not only a man of God, but also a performer of great skill; and his sermon was delivered with such power of emphasis and illustration, such infinite variation of tone and texture and sing-song Afrikaans, that though I could not understand a word it left me both chastened and edified. Sometimes during the service all the men stood up, leaving the women kneeling in attitudes of soul-searing repentance, and when we left the church and filed into the street, to the echoes of a last fruity amen from the predikant, we all looked thoroughly and comfortably ashamed of ourselves, as sinners should (and none more than me, for I had spent the previous evening in a cloud of burgundy).

For there *are* sinners in Bloemfontein. Far less chastened and penitent than my congregation are some of the citizens you may see gobbling steaks in the gloomy restaurants of the city. The men are plumpish and bulge-eyed, and many of them wear blazers and open-necked shirts, and drink brandy, the national beverage of South Africa; and the women are apt to be blowsy and over-dressed, with a superfluity of ornaments and a baffling variety of tastes, so that I once observed a courtesan in a Bloemfontein hotel wearing a magnificent mink wrap over a pink cardigan and a golfing skirt. For all the puritanical fervour of the city, it has an undersoil of locked doors, delinquence and hidden salacity. Sometimes the 'ducktails', the young bloods of the Union, riot in the streets for the gratification of their spike-heeled admirers. Often there is a sudden swift swish in a hotel corridor, or the cautious sliding of a bolt. In the nature reserve of Naval Hill a camel stalks through the scrub with an expression of undying licentiousness. In the zoo a lion and a tiger once miscegenated, and produced a celebrated family of ligers. It is strange that so zealous a city should carry this suggestion of hidden habits, but possibly only natural: Bloemfontein was founded, so they say, by a crew of cheerful and unscrupulous ne'er-do-wells, and it has a history of bloodshed and galli-vanting.

Life there is leavened, too, by the presence of one of the best and wittiest newspapers in Africa, *The Friend*. It is a happy paradox that this English-language journal exists at all. Not a single Opposition member sits in the Provincial Council or represents any Free State constituency in the national Parliament: but Bloemfontein has old British connections, and perhaps a third of its population is still English-speaking, so that in the very centre of the Free State, the most irrefragably Afrikaner province of them all, a newspaper is to be found vehemently opposing the excesses of Afrikaner chauvinism. *The Friend* has proud memories of the Boer War, for when the British captured Bloemfontein Rudyard Kipling became its temporary editor, and stamped it, or at least its reputation, indelibly with his genius. Perhaps he inspired its original liberal impetus, for at the height of the war, when the Boer general Joubert died, Kipling printed in *The Friend* the stanza:

> *Later shall rise a People, sane and great,*
> *Forged in strong fires, by equal war made one,*
> *Telling old battles over without hate*
> *—Not least his name shall pass from Sire to son*

—which was, though clumsy, a notably broad-minded sentiment to express in the middle of so vicious a conflict. *The Friend* has several flourishing subsidiaries, and they say that more newspapers and magazines are printed each week in Bloemfontein than in any other city of the same size in the world (but be careful of these statistics, for when South Africans say a city has 40,000 inhabitants, they mean 40,000 *whites*; just as the Arabian princeling, observed ushering his harem of forty portly ladies aboard a smallish airliner, contemptuously brushed aside the bourgeois suggestion that *women* had to be counted, too).

In uncomfortable proximity to this gay and caustic newspaper is the celebrated Women's Monument, one of the great sights of the Orange Free State. The Voortrekker Monument celebrates one of the mystical props of Afrikaner nationalism: this perpetuates the agonies of another, for it honours the thousands of women and children who died in British concentration camps during the Boer War (or the Anglo-Boer War, or the Freedom War, as the Afrikaner patriots understandably prefer to call it). I do not know the truth about the concentration camps, whether—as the Afrikaners say—the British were unnecessarily harsh in confining non-combatants and devastating the countryside foot by foot; or whether these policies were unavoidable, and conducted as humanely as possible. It is undeniable that several thousand people died in the camps, in the heart-rending winter of the High Veldt, but it is also true that the chief cause of death among the British soldiery was disease rather than battle. Whatever the truth, it can hardly be contested that the Bloemfontein monument, the wailing wall of Afrikanerdom, helps to keep alive the malignancies between Boer and Briton: and it is difficult to escape the suspicion that this has become one of its purposes.

The monument crowns the summit of a hillock outside Bloemfontein, a tall and noble obelisk, with a gigantic female figure in a poke bonnet standing against its stone, and the graves of three or four notables (among them the Englishwoman Emily Hobhouse) grouped around its base. There are nearly always Afrikaner pilgrims here, standing before the obelisk with their hats in their hands: if the Voortrekker Monument is the Mecca of Afrikanerdom, this is its Medina. Nearby there is a museum containing relics of the war, from conference tables to rifles and watercolours by Miss Hobhouse. The most horrific exhibit is a photograph of an *impi* of black men deliberately armed by the British to fight the Boers. I have never seen a sorrier troop of horsemen, straggling in inept procession across a plain, and indeed I am told they were an abysmal failure; but to the Afrikaner this arming of Africans was a deliberate affront to the divine order, and it is significant that never again, not in the burning moments of world crisis or the brooding day of the satellites, has a black man in South Africa been given a gun.

Tucked away in some inner vaults, the museum allegedly possesses evidence confirming one of the more persistent Afrikaner atrocity stories: the legend, still tirelessly propagated, that in those notorious concentration camps the British larded the porridge with ground glass, to ensure the extermination of a few more innocents. I asked if I might see this, but the woman in charge told me that the evidence was not yet ready for presentation. It had to be properly prepared, you know. 'Why not throw it away?' I said. 'Even if it's true, it can only do harm to South Africa, what's the use of keeping it?' At this a queer thing happened. That woman looked hard at me, her fine blue eyes penetrating mine, and then, quite suddenly, she seemed to freeze. It was as if some outside force, some icy guardian governess, had tapped her on the shoulder and shrivelled her muscles. A resolutely vacuous look spread over her face, blank and forbidding, and I realized that an impenetrable shutter had been lowered between us. Some old spiky instinct, bred by resentment out of history, had been touched on a sensitive nerve and reacted accordingly.

For in Bloemfontein the Afrikaner is still jealous of his past, and proud of the admirably governed little republic which gave this city its days of glory. Lord Bryce called it a model republic, and many a Bloemfontein citizen looks back to its palmy decades with a sort of vicarious nostalgia. To this day the Free State remains the least spoilt, the most pastoral, the simplest and horniest of the South African provinces. It is still a place of peasant traits and old-fashioned hospitality, and if ever you attend a rustic wedding in the Orange Free State, you will realize how close the Afrikaner can be to the world of the

Breughels and the old Dutch masters. The reception is held in
the church hall, and the room is packed, and hot with robust
gaiety. At the top table sit the bride and groom, flushed and
rotund, she in an ornate white headdress, he intolerably corseted
in black. Here are the bride's parents, wrinkled and sharp of
face; and here also the two small bridesmaids, their plump
country figures wrapped in pink and blue, posed self-consciously
beside a potted palm. Big black servants scurry about with
cold drinks and sweetmeats. 'It's all done to plan,' says your
host complacently. 'All the tables are numbered, you see, and
the invitations are numbered too, so that every one knows just
where to sit—no confusion, you see, no pushing or shoving,
everyone can have a good time.' And indeed everyone does.
Now and then somebody makes a speech, in a loud, assertive
but generally disregarded monologue; and the bride and bride-
groom sometimes simper at each other, at the demand of ama-
teur photographers; and a hubbub of enjoyment and mastica-
tion fills the hall. Each trestle table makes a party of its own, and
eats its pastries with gusto, and shouts cheerfully for the Africans with the drinks; and the whole scene is warm and homely
and animated, with the sheen of red velvet dresses, the fizz of
bottled pop, smiling weathered faces, white satin, excited little
girls and a smell of flowers and scent and sandwiches.

8

NEW GOLD

Ten years ago Bloemfontein was even more provincial of manner than it is now. The Orange Free State has always been the Cinderella of the South African provinces, and long ago became accustomed to sitting in the chimney corner knitting woollies. Landlocked and harsh, an unaccommodating prairie state, it subsisted largely on farming and piety and proud Boer memories: and the erosion that is perpetually gnawing at the Union's soil attacked the Free State with especial ferocity. The old grasslands and flowers of the veldt had long since surrendered to to-day's prickly bushes, drab shrubs and dusty gulleys, and many a stout Afrikaner farmer had sold his stock, packed his old car, and driven away to find work in the cities. The biggest industrial plant was the railway workshop at Bloemfontein (here, as in America, the railways make a potent contribution to the ethos of the state). There was practically no manufacturing and precious little capital investment. Next door the Transvaalers basked in the munificence of their natural resources; but the Orange Free State was the dowdiest of poor relations.

All has changed, and a good deal more money now flows through the arteries of Bloemfontein, and warms the cockles of many an arid Afrikaner heart. The foundation of South Africa's astonishing wealth has always been gold, exploited for half a century in a crescent reef running through the Witwatersrand. So many hundreds of millions of tons of ore have been moved from this monumental reef, over the years, that its resources are now obviously wilting. Mines have to be driven ever deeper, and though the South African subterrain is abnormally cool,

71

this nevertheless entails more expensive cooling systems, less efficient labour, and less economical mining. So during the war the mining companies intensified their search for an extension to the reef. The theory was that the Witwatersrand reef was one rim of a basin: that as it deepened towards the south-west, so it would emerge again somewhere else as another outcrop. Some authorities scoffed at this notion, and maintained that the reef petered out; others said that, if it did extend farther towards the south-west, it merely plunged deeper into the earth (12,000 feet is probably the deepest a gold mine can be worked in South Africa). But the Anglo-American Corporation, taking a chance, worked farther into the Free State and finally sank a borehole in an outcrop at Odendaalsrus, a minute farming community ninety miles from Bloemfontein. A fabulous discovery was then made, and Cinderella instantly prepared for metamorphosis. Not only was there gold at 4,500 feet—half the depth of the deepest Rand mines: the ore was also 300 times richer than the average ore of the Rand. All of a sudden the Orange Free State found itself in possession of perhaps the richest and biggest and most convenient goldfield on earth.

Thus I was able, in the winter of 1957, to experience the epilogue of a gold rush. By the time I arrived at the site of Odendaalsrus, scarcely a trace remained of that lucky hamlet, and there was nothing to be seen of those bearded hoary prospectors, nuggets in hand, whose ribaldry still lingers tenaciously about the diggings of the Comstock Lode and the surviving gilded saloons of the Rand. The fortunate farmers of the place had disappeared with their royalties, and that dreary patch of veldt, monotonous beyond words, was burgeoning with mine-hoists and compounds and spanking new towns. Twelve gold mines were already working, and a breath-taking quantity of gold was leaving each morning, guarded by a single burly detective, on board the elderly Lodestar aircraft which linked the new field with Main Street, the City of London and the ultimate vaults of Fort Knox. This, the newest of the world's great gold-fields, was not exploited by the myriad shoving individualists of earlier discoveries, but was organized with authority by the

Johannesburg magnates and the Union Government. There had never been a gold rush quite like this: in nine years Anglo-American alone spent £100 m. on shaft-sinking, and this legendary concern later established six new gold mines all at the same time, an astonishing project. Mining leases are granted by the Government, which is paid a rent according to the esoteric formula: $Y = 30 - \frac{180}{X}$, where X is the ratio of profit to recovery, and Y is the percentage of profit payable to the Government. It has been estimated, Heaven knows how, that the yield of the new goldfield will eventually amount to £4,344,000,000: so, as a friendly official remarked to me one morning, 'You can work out the Government's potential profit for yourself, if you happen to know the value of X.'

Elaborate though the workings were by 1957, there was still something of the pioneering spirit to the Free State goldfield, a little of that frontier virility that is one of the compensations of life in South Africa. An entirely new urban complex, as the sociologists would put it, had swamped the old bucolics of Odenraalsrus, but there remained some sense of brashness and gusto and violent change, as befits an Eldorado. A few short years before there had been virtually nothing here, only scattered homesteads and some dirt roads. There had been no electricity, no piped water, no tarmac, no railway, no local administration—nothing but the dour farmers and their scrubby veldt. Now the mining companies and the brisk business opportunists had built the township of Welkom. Nothing in it was more than ten years old, but it already had a population of 60,000 and was the second largest city in the province. When I arrived there, to be sure, it was a welter of mud after a savage rainstorm, and the big American cars of the mine-men were floundering in the muck, and the little English ones had unanimously given up, and stood there forlornly with their bonnets open. But generally it is quite a comfortable place, with a Greek café where you can buy caviare, and a general store where you can buy any perfume under the sun, and an excellent hotel where a German baron once told me, with an old-school sniff, that the black Bantu was no better and no worse than his estate manager in pre-war

Pomerania—'if you gave him a bath, he kept his coal in it: if you built him a coal-shed, he used it for his perpetual fornications. Bah!' There is a bright, impulsive, acquisitive feeling to it all, very stimulating to experience, and instinct with carpet-baggers as well as capitalists.

There is also at Welkom one of the most magnificent hospitals I have ever seen. Anglo-American built it for their African employees, and dutifully named it the Ernest Oppenheimer Hospital. Here those black mineworkers who need patching up, come to be scrupulously patched; and lavish is the equipment, and skilful the treatment they are given. Here is an African immersed in an electric bath, all trussed up with harnesses and pulleys, and flapping his arms about in the warm water like a great black seal at sea, the pink soles of his feet flowing like phosphorescence, and his face contorted with effort. (Black men have pink palms and soles, so the Africans say, because when the world was young and grimy the white men used all the water, and the Africans had only enough left for a lick and a polish.) Here is a crisp young African nurse, with a smile like snow, and here a little English physiotherapist proudly shows you his American gadgets. The white nurses are all nuns. It is difficult to induce first-class doctors or nurses to come to Welkom, boom town though it is, so Sir Ernest Oppenheimer himself thought of inviting a conventual order to undertake the nursing duties; they perform them with an air of clinical sweetness, and have their own hostel next door, and a tennis-court on which, I am told, they very often hitch up their habits for a few spirited sets. There is a big women's wing, but only two or three languid expectant mothers occupy its grandeurs: the company wanted to establish a settled African society at Welkom, with wives and families, but the Government insisted on maintaining the compound system in its entirety. The critics say, anyway, that such good works as these are so much hypocritical blarney, that the companies are thinking only of their efficiency, that when a case of silicosis is diagnosed the miner is not cured, merely sent home: but it is only fair to recognize the quality of so fine a hospital, whatever the motives that animate it.

NEW GOLD

Anglo-American have also tried, for one reason or another, to humanize their compounds in the new goldfields, by introducing grand new dining-halls and cafeteria systems, and calling them hostels. This has not been a wild success. The miners do not like eating in a dining-room and collecting their food ready cooked; they much prefer to feed in the smoky intimacy of their own dormitories, crouched hugger-mugger around an open fire, and spitting when they feel like it. The cheerful daintiness of these new buildings, their almost spinsterish ambiance, does not yet appeal to the earthy tribesman; and poor Anglo-American, for all their progressive views, find that the miners prefer to sign on down the road, where a rival group provides them with all the old communal discomforts. (Many an unexpected paradox pesters the opinions of the visitor to South Africa, and sometimes healthily befuddles his preconceptions.) And for myself, I view with some slight scepticism the elaborate methods by which this company tests the aptitude of its recruits, keeping its examination rooms at a constant temperature 'because we find the psychological reaction varies according to the warmth and coolth': the story goes that when a distinguished financier undertook the tests, just for fun, he was graded as suitable for sanitation work, a job usually done by the gumboot dancers.

Here, as in the Rand, most of the lower-grade white workers are Afrikaners, most of the senior men English-speaking; and an interesting, friendly, bright-eyed community they form. The competition in their profession is intense, and the plums of such a vital, expanding goldfield as this are succulent indeed. The mine managers live grandly, in pompous houses with rock gardens and swimming-pools, and are the aristocracy of Welkom; the bright young men of the management live in a spick-and-span hostel, complaining only of a shortage of girls, and very often flying to Johannesburg for the week-end. Trade unionism and colour prejudice apart, there is very little stuffiness in the South African mining profession. One of my guides at Welkom was a young man of singular charm, but of tendencies which I can only describe as inclining towards the delicate, and I won-

dered how easily he had adapted himself to the hearty world of
the mining engineers: I was pleasantly surprised, for he had not
adapted himself at all, but had instead so convinced those hard-
headed technicians of his ability and integrity that they were
eating out of his scented hand. I detected, though, some slight
antipathy towards new recruits from England. 'The very first
question they ask', one man told me, 'is how much their pension
is going to be; and the very first answer they get is . . .'—but I
must not quote him, for we are in the Orange Free State, and a
predikant may be listening.

In some ways (though distinctly not in others) South Africa
is positively swamped in good fortune. There seems no possibility, just at the moment, that gold will lose its place in the
financial arrangements of the world—to modern civilization it
has just the same undeserved significance as it had to the sages
of ancient China or the unknown administrators of Zimbabwe.
But even if it did lose its meaning, this great new goldfield would
not be altogether destitute: for it also harbours immense
reserves of uranium, the raw material of the atomic era. It was
during the war that the South Africans, in elaborate secrecy,
began to exploit their uranium deposits, until now they are one
of the principal providers of the western world, and possess the
biggest reserves of all. This is very convenient. The uranium content of these reefs is not high, and the mines might not be
economically workable in peacetime if only uranium were extracted: but as it is, the uranium comes out with the gold, and the
companies simply recover it from the slimes that are produced
anyway by the gold-processing plants. There are even deposits of
uranium to be extracted from the old slime dumps littering the
face of the Rand, which is rather like discovering gold sovereigns
hidden among your great-grandmother's stays in the attic.
There are no mining costs, and the market is not only assured,
but downright greedy—all South African uranium goes to an
Anglo-American organization called the Combined Development Agency. The price is secret and is fixed by ten-year agree-
ments.

Until recently the processes of this new industry were shuttered in secrecy. People peered with awe at the convoluted pipes of the uranium plants, and no doubt the occasional spy did his best to penetrate them. Barbed wire surrounded the installations, armed sentries guarded them, and when the uranium slime was sent off to its final treatment on the West Rand, it travelled in shabby grey unmarked tanker trucks. (At Los Alamos, when they were devising the first atomic bomb, the local know-alls said it was going to be some vast globular vehicle which could be rolled across the countryside crushing whole battalions. In South Africa, I learnt, tedious men in saloon bars used to tell their deluded listeners that these tanker trucks were filled with helium, for a series of inter-continental dirigibles being assembled secretly in the Karoo.) By the time I visited my first uranium plant they had become disarmingly matter-of-fact about it all. The man in charge was only thirty, and his staff was at once relaxed and impressively thorough. They told me they had tested their ore for dangerous radioactivity by mixing a dog's food with uranium powder; nothing happened to the animal, they said, except that he put on weight 'and something seemed to be different about his bark'. I cannot pretend to have mastered the technique by which uranium oxide is extracted from the gold slime, but I am assured that exactly the same process has been developed by the Russians, which is the reason why I was allowed to see it at all. Most of it seems to be controlled by automation, and it has something to do with a series of enormous rotating cylinders, around which the slime revolves stickily like cake mixture in a mould; and something to do with a series of gigantic vats, in which big metal agitators swirl the stuff about; and something to do with some outdoor reservoirs in which an unpleasant glutinous substance is left to fester and thicken in the sunshine, like puddles after a flood. The predominant colour of this process is yellow. The fluid in those huge vats is yellowish, and at the end of our tour my guide produces for me, with a conjuror's panache, a small bottle of minute yellow crystals, rather like sands from the Isle of Wight. 'There you are,' he said, wiping his hands and locking the cupboard, 'that's what makes the bombs go off!'

NEW GOLD

All this new bustling activity, this boring and mining and processing, has revivified the Orange Free State and given it a new importance in the councils of the Union. It no longer stands quite so isolated and introspective among its erosions. There are people who say that the entire processes of government should now be concentrated in Bloemfontein, 'the centre city'; there are others who believe that before very long the Free State goldfield will be as rich and populated and celebrated as the Rand itself. And only occasionally will you hear a plaintive Afrikaner voice regretting the arrival of the airstrips, the gold mines and the caviare, and muttering a mystic incantation about the smoke from the next man's chimney.

9

AFRIKANERDOM

For myself, I cherish a secret sympathy for such *sotto voce* sentiments, unprogressive though they may be, just as I confess to a begrudging affection and admiration for the Afrikaner national character. There is nobody quite like the Afrikaner, so frowardly disagreeable as the young city-dweller can be, so grand and so simple as the old-school Boer patriarch. It is all too easy to weary of the cruder sort, the grumpy shopkeeper, the overbearing bus conductor, the niggling official, the coarse-grained policeman, the greasy hypocritical predikant: but you can hardly help warming to the guileless hospitality of the countryman, whatever his views on Kaffirs and creation, and here and there you may meet a man so blue of eye, so shaggy of demeanour and disposition, so bold and spacious even in his bigotry, that you are transported instantly to the great days of the Boer commandos, when Smuts and his bands of imperturbable irregulars roamed the Karoo and the High Veldt. Splendid are the Afrikaner qualities; and there is even a harsh merit to the chauvinism of the nationalists, the hankering for a dead past, the racial pride and religious rigidity, the stubbornness of that woman in the Bloemfontein museum, the virile eccentricity of the clergyman who drew his shotgun on the jay-walker.

I was once driving through the Transvaal when I noticed a small obelisk on a hillock beside the road. I stopped and climbed a little path to inspect it, and beside its plinth I found two men crouching in what seemed to be silent homage or meditation. One of them, squatting a few feet behind the other, was a black man in rags: he wore no shoes, his old khaki greatcoat was torn and dirty, his hair was matted and unkempt, and his eyes now and then flickered away from the monument and over the dreary countryside that surrounded us. The other was an old white farmer. He wore an unbuttoned waterproof jacket. A linen hat slouched about his ears, and a mass of curly hair lay down his neck and oozed over his collar. As I approached he turned to look at me, and I found myself gazing into the bluest and clearest and hardest pair of eyes I had ever seen. The face that smiled at me was round and sunburnt, and engraved with innumerable deep lines—the kind of face you may sometimes see on old-fashioned Iowa farms, or even occasionally in the boardrooms of tabulator factories in Cedar Rapids: but the body was as lithe and stringy as gristle, a muscular combination of grace and age. 'Who's the memorial to?' I asked him, as we shook hands. 'One of our great Boer generals,' he replied, and added simply: 'I'm his son, I look after the place.'

So I met, almost as in a reincarnation, one of the legendary Boers we read about, those hardy champions of prejudice and resolution. I disagreed with almost everything this man said: I thought his bigotry often bordered upon the insane; I found his every thought, his every value, almost diametrically opposed to mine; I could see that he might develop, given half a chance, into an appalling bore; and yet I have seldom warmed more readily to a chance acquaintance or felt more confident in his honesty. He gave me a packet of biltong, prepared by his wife, and we sat in the back of his car and drank some lukewarm coffee out of a thermos flask, while his raggety servant weeded the path to the obelisk. He suffered from no false modesty ('I'm always *giving*, it's one of my failings') and he held violent and generally unshakable opinions on almost every subject. Why, only a few days ago, he told me, he had sent a telegram to the Commonwealth Conference in London, warning the assembled Prime Ministers that Communism, Catholicism and Jewry were secretly allied in a campaign to overthrow western civilization. 'But they're blind, you know, *blind*. Churchill was just the same. I sent him a cable in 1941—it cost me £7—to warn him that Russia was Antichrist. But he disregarded it. He never answered at all. I suppose he read it?' said that old Boer, unscrewing the thermos flask. 'What do you think?'

So we chatted pleasantly, and during the next half-hour he assured me that the British were the first to bomb civilians; that he didn't believe in the existence of Nazi concentration camps; that the Kaiser had, after all, sent a friendly telegram to Kruger; that the Communists were financed by international Jewry; that the natives would never be civilized; that Shakespeare was Bacon, the 46th Psalm proved it; that his mother had eaten fungus in a British concentration camp; that the hydrogen bomb was Antichrist; that he had sent a cable to President Eisenhower telling him so; that his wife was the loveliest woman in Africa; and that if ever I came that way again I was welcome to stay at his farm and eat his biltong and disagree with his arguments for as long as I liked. It was a pleasure, said he, to meet a visitor from England, and that reminded him, had I seen the incontrovertible evidence at Bloemfontein concerning the ground glass and the porridge?

This was a Boer in the grand manner. Another kind, though no less rooted in his convictions, is rather more niggling and petulant, nearer the Welsh than the Scots. In the Orange Free State I once had tea with a well-known Afrikaner educationalist. We sat in his study beside the fire, surrounded by books of theology, political theory and general uplift, and supervised by an enormous portrait of President Kruger, so dominating and intrusive that I could almost feel his whiskers tickling the back of my neck. My host was a little man with round spectacles, precise and rather pedantic, but somehow indefinably squirmy; and sometimes, no less than the general's son, he made remarks that in almost any other environment would seem a little dotty.

'Well, Professor,' said I, 'it does seem to me that you have a most disagreeable racial problem in your country. Have you any thoughts on the subject?'

'Mmm,' mused the academic, 'it *is* a problem, that's perfectly true. But you see, for hundreds of generations the natives were lying plunged deep in *sin*—and it is *sin*, Mr. Morris, that drove men into their different races. The religion that overcomes the heart of man, that struggles against its sinful infirmity, decides his civilization. Look at the difference,' he went on kindly, licking the butter from his fingers, 'between Catholics and Protestants! The high civilization of Europe is a product of our Protestant faith. (You are a Protestant, of course? Good.) Look at the Dutch, and the Germans, and the Scandinavians—ha, ha, and the English too, for all our differences!'

Yes, I said hastily, but how did he feel about the principle of apartheid?

'All those who stand for the principle of apartheid go to the Old Testament for their texts. All those who stand for equality, for a mingling of the races, yes, for a coffee-coloured society— all those who stand for *integration* quote from the New! This is a tragedy of our times. We are responsible to God for our policies. Whether the natives can ever become politically adult depends upon what is going on in their hearts—those poor hearts plunged through the centuries in dreadful sin. If the native cooperates, he may be given the vote in six or eight generations. If he doesn't he may never get it. My dear Mr. Morris, on our family farm we *loved* our natives, we were brought up to love them because they were real Christians, generations under the word of God, and they knew their place.'

And at this point, I say without conceit, I deftly changed the conversation, and we spent the rest of the evening amiably discussing inessentials, until with the unfailing courtesy of the educated Afrikaner he walked with me to his garden gate and raised his hat in an ornate farewell. He may have been misguided, but in his way he was very kind.

We have already tasted the hospitality of the simpler Afrikaner countryman, and sipped his sweet coffee, and suspected we heard the cracking of his whip in the backyard: but no impression of South Africa would be complete without a glimpse of the rock-bottom Afrikaner poor white, who contributes powerfully to the tone of the place and does much to endanger its future. The Union is a place of glorious landscapes, smiling bank balances, and incorrigibly cheerful Africans. It is also, alas, one of the rudest countries I have ever visited, and for this the lower-class urbanized Afrikaner is chiefly to blame. Few experiences in modern travel are more disheartening than asking a man of this type for information, or foolishly engaging him in small talk, or inquiring his opinion on the United Nations. Refractory is the face he will then turn upon you, and thick the accent with which, after a heavy pause for the assembly of his prejudices, he will do his best to humiliate you. If you happen to be black he will probably throw in a curse or an insult; if you are English, he will pretend he does not understand your language; but even if you are a fellow-countryman, a fellow-subject of the Volkswil, he may well be just as surly. He is often a man excised from a rural background and thrown suddenly into the rush of urban life; and he does not accept the metamorphosis easily.

I once travelled across the Transkei by bus, together with an elderly farmer of resolutely English stock. It was really a mail-truck, but there was a little compartment for passengers, with a single bench seat; and the driver and his mate had their own places in front. On our journey, though, the driver's mate chose to sit with us in the passengers' cabin, and moreover to seize one of the window seats; and I remember with a distaste bordering upon loathing his presence with us during that long, bumpy and arid journey. He sat there frumpishly with his peaked cap on the back of his head and his shirt-sleeves rolled up almost to his shoulders. He wore grubby khaki shorts and gym shoes, and he propped his long hairy legs on the partition in front of him as, sucking a cigarette and occasionally picking his nose, he sprawled beside us reading a comic. Once or twice he brusquely demanded our tickets. Sometimes he jumped noisily out to deliver the mail at a trading station or a farm-house. Always, with a contemptuous stare at the farmer and a glare at me, he hogged that window seat again, and filled our modest compartment with his tobacco smoke, and lounged there in an attitude of unspeakable arrogance. 'What a despicable creature!' announced the farmer after a hundred miles of this. 'Young man, why don't you go and sit with your colleague in front, or doesn't he like you either?' And with a sullen sniff and a wipe of his nose, that unpleasant bus conductor rose slowly to his feet, banged the door behind him, and climbed sulkily into his proper place, muttering. 'Dreadful person,' said the farmer. 'And these are to be our masters, are they? Well, we'll see about that! Ha!' And he buried himself in his book, *With Gun and Theodolite Through the Karoo.*

It is not simply nationalism that provokes the disgruntlement of such a young Afrikaner. To be sure, he has been educated by Church and Volk to fight for the supremacy of his race within the Union, and to remember with resentment the old British misdemeanours—the Jameson Raid, the two Boer Wars, the concentration camps, the attempts to stifle the Afrikaans language, the superiority complex of British South Africans, British monopolies in mining and commerce, the blind assumption that a South African is necessarily a sort of hot-house Briton. He shares all the racial fervour of those Transvaal agriculturists, if his religious views are less pronounced than my dogmatic professor's. But it is more than mere frustrated patriotism that makes him grumpy. His is a people that has been isolated, for one reason and another, for a century or more; and he feels, as his father did, that the wide world is not only strange, but inherently hostile. Nobody speaks his language except the two million people of his own race. He has no links with Europe and America. His only home is here in Africa. Almost everywhere else the stern Calvinist creed of his upbringing has been softened by humanism, and his unyielding pride of race and history is sadly out of tune with the internationalism of the time. He is testy of criticism, suspicious of mockery and condescension, quick to anger and difficult to please. Moreover, he is extraordinarily unmalleable. To the Afrikaner, often enough, everything is permanently tabulated and classified, and separated by watertight bulkheads. You are either black or white. You may either live in this street, or in that. Things are either absolutely right or hopelessly wrong. If you are an Afrikaner you must be a whole-hog Afrikaner nationalist. If you are an Englishman you must be snubbed in buses or told about the fungus. Nothing must be blurred or smudged or flexible or half-way, and the pressure towards conformity within the Volk is forceful and un-relenting. (A university lecturer told me that she never asked her Afrikaner students to discuss the rejection of Falstaff. 'They think he's shamefully undisciplined, so they don't see anything paradoxical in it!') Worst of all, the Afrikaner feels that when it comes to dealing with the black African, only our Johnny can be in step. 'You blerry foreigners,' they will say, 'man, you don't know what you're talking about. Ach, man, these Kaffirs are only one better than the animals! Then you people come along, a month in the country and you think you know better than us. Here's your ticket, man, there's the bus.'

Very often, though, during my stay in South Africa I was heartened by the feeling that all this was slowly changing. Time and again some instinct told me that the frozen façade of Afri-kanerdom was beginning to thaw, that the stream of ideas from the west was already (with a muffled clang) striking the Afrikaner consciousness. My professor would find a hundred thousand Afrikaners ready to ridicule his theories. I met innumerable young Afrikaners who had been abroad, for holiday or for study, and who had come home again puzzled, if not emanci-pated. In Accra I once encountered an Afrikaner business-man who had just, for the first time in his life, danced with a black girl. 'I went and sat down', he said, 'and I waited for the reaction to set in. There was bound to be some reaction, I thought. But d'you know, nothing happened, nothing at all, and I'm going to write straight off to my Mum and tell her so!' For the moment the Volk is still rigid and unbending, governed by the complexes of a conquered or beleaguered race; but the Afrikaner is now master of the Union, and as he gains in con-fidence perhaps his views will mellow.

And if you have any doubts about the potential of this re-markable people, introduce yourself to a renegade Afrikaner, one who has rejected the standard values and dogmas of his race. He is probably an ex-serviceman (although the Afrikaner ex-tremists supported the Nazi cause, sometimes with sabotage and skullduggery, most of the volunteers for the South African forces were Afrikaner, not British). He is certainly bitingly intelligent. He necessarily has guts, because declaring for the progressive cause subjects him to all kinds of subtle pressures, social, economic and professional. His humour is advanced and caustic. He is unlikely to be one of your topsy-turvy liberals, with their soggy devotion to the underdog, and he tempers his political idealism with a reasonable thread of self-interest. One such man was Jan Hofmeyr, a politician whose memory is remembered with devotion everywhere in the Union. Another was Deneys Reitz, who wrote so marvellously of the Boer commandos, and rose to represent his country in London. It was only by the saddest and smallest of margins that the detribalized Afrikaners, at one period of history, failed to achieve unity among English and Afrikaner in the Union, and thus pave the way to partnership between all its races, black and white: and sometimes, for all the moanings of the Jeremiahs and the crazy excesses of the nationalists, I have the heartening feeling that they may achieve it yet.

'So I sent a telegram to Krushchev,' continued that old patriarch between mouthfuls, 'but *he* never answered either. There's no manners in the world nowadays, no manners at all.'

10

INTELLECTUALS

If there is ever a revival of the 'twin stream' policy, which animated the Reitzes and Hofmeyers and Smutses of thirty years ago, it may well occur through the efforts of the South African intellectuals. Both the Afrikaners and the British have fairly flourishing cultures of their own: but there is also a climate of thought that is common to them both, and recognizably national. A significant number of those who consider themselves simply South Africans, no more, no less, are people who deal in matters of the mind, and thereby realize the futility of petty nationalisms. Many of the best thinkers of white South Africa (and make no mistake, this is a highly intelligent community) manage to stand astride the races, and would, were it not for a name and sometimes a persuasion, defy any close genetical analysis.

This limited coalition the nationalists have done their best to destroy, by injecting politics and nationalism and the excesses of apartheid into intellectual life. In their unyielding attempts to separate the alleged goats from the assumed sheep, they have introduced measures to ensure that only the Government has any say in the education of the black African. Nearly all the native schools must now be officially run, and a new Bill will prevent any African from attending the three South African universities that are now inter-racial. People say that the new state universities being established for Africans will provide only an education for subservience. Certainly, since they are to be under government supervision of the most direct kind, there will be little political free-thinking in their campuses and common-rooms, and none of that grand liberty of action that is the hall-mark of a real university. For myself, I suspect the students will learn as much as they ever did, and there are good arguments for an education that will fit them, in particular, for work among their own peoples: but it is hypocritical to pretend that these will be true universities in our sense of the word, and there is something especially despicable about racial differentiation in matters of the intellect.

Because of these stresses and intentions, you may see in South Africa one of the classic symptoms of authoritarianism: the spectacle of academics and intellectuals publicly protesting against the policies of government—not simply the angry young men of English dissatisfaction, or the twisted young Jews who gnaw at their grievances in the American faculties, but academics of the gravest and most distinguished kind. The liberal universities have fought bravely and frankly against the Universities Apartheid Bill and kindred measures, and there have been ominous reminders of the Burning of the Books, of the struggle of the Soviet biologists, of McCarthyism and the Inquisition—coupled with, to descend from the historic to the banal, very distinct reminders of the campaign against a by-pass through Christ Church Meadows. South Africa is not in general a stylish country: but it is an unhappy one, and such conflicts as this therefore have their moments of nobility. I was once in Cape Town when the faculty and student body of the university marched in solemn phalanx through the streets of the city in protest against the government's policies. It was a sad and unforgettable sight. In the South African environment, so riddled with paradoxes and improbabilities, nothing seems very surprising: but it is difficult to imagine the entire academic body of Oxford, Cambridge or Harvard parading through the populace with such earnest political purpose.

Several thousand men and women marched through Cape Town that winter morning, watched by a few impassive policemen, applauded by a little raggle-taggle assembly lining the route in a condition of baffled sympathy. Anywhere else in the world the procession might have smacked of the ludicrous or the theatrical, so implacably grim was the expression on everyone's face, and so subtly reminiscent was the demonstration of some ambitious but disheartened seaside carnival. First came two girls all in white, meant to be significant of intellectual purity, in fact instantly evocative of drum-majorettes at ball games. Then, to the beat of side-drums, a group of elderly scholars in the robes of their distinction: some red, some purple, some a flaming blue. Their clever craggy faces were frozen in earnestness, and they moved with a sombre and determined rhythm. One was lame, and carried a shooting-stick. All stared straight before them, stern and unsmiling, like angry begowned sphinxes. Lesser professors and lecturers followed, bespectacled or sporty, in double-vent jackets or scholarly pin-stripe, chesty or round-shouldered, tired or eager, marching four abreast with their arms swinging, like some unlikely but obscurely formidable battalion of irregulars; and far down the street behind them moved the innumerable ranks of students, trailing away in diminishing gradations of discipline, until the girls at the back were chatting seriously as they walked, now and then breaking into a hurried trot to keep up with the others. There were thousands of men and hundreds of women, an African now and then, a few Malays from the Cape Asiatic community, here a girl in a flouncy striped skirt, there a resolute blue-stocking with her hair done up in what appeared to be silver paper. The police looked on silently. The traffic waited. Swinging its arms, beating its drums, thinking its angry thoughts, that great assembly advanced step by step towards Table Mountain, alive with an indignation rather more righteous than *saevo*.

Perhaps such a thing could only happen in South Africa. Though this is a country plagued with suggestions of autocracy, for white people it is a fairly free country still: gnarled professors with shooting-sticks, idealistic girls with silver paper curlers are still at liberty to express their discontent. Fortunately there remains much respect for learning in South Africa. The straggly crowds that lined those streets were partly apathetic, partly mystified, partly in disagreement, but never derisive. Beside me a middle-aged lady in a fluffy blue tam-o'-shanter lifted her hand in a V-for-Victory sign, a befuddled gesture of support. A young man with thick spectacles asked me if it was an election campaign. I heard one bright shopgirl say to another, more in surprise than in rancour: 'Look at the Kaffirs, then, all mixed up with the rest! Did you ever?' Nobody showed any ferocious enthusiasm for the cause, but everyone respected the intensity and emotion of the occasion, and watched quietly as the professors marched by.

There is veneration, too, for the learned men of the various churches. We have seen how powerful are the different sects of the Dutch Reformed sects: other churches, too, especially the Anglican, play an important role in the political affairs of the country, and there is some common ground of opinion among intelligent churchmen of all kinds, from the Calvinist intelligentsia to the Catholics. As the universities are threatened by the Universities Apartheid Bill, so the churchmen have protested against a clause in another law under which it can be declared illegal for black people to enter white churches. This madness has even displeased the more conservative synods of the Dutch Church, let alone the handful of advanced and outspoken predikants who are among the most hopeful figures in the Union to-day. If segregation in learning is an insult, segregation in worship surely smacks of the blasphemous, for all the smiling sophistries of that country minister in the Transvaal. Outside one big Anglican church there stands a defiant poster: 'This church is open to welcome men and women of *all races* to *all services* at *all times*.' For once, so irrational is this milieu, sanity has to go into italics: and the Anglican clergy is prepared to defy the law, and risk the possible penalty of flogging, if the Government ever tries to implement the church clause. (But there is hypocrisy in this, as in every South African dispute: many an Anglican who protests with vehemence against the law would loathe to find a black man kneeling beside him at the Communion rail.)

Partly because of these politico-spiritual disputes, some of the most important liberal spokesmen in South Africa are clergymen. Some are idealists of noble but impractical fervour, others men of solid stature who see themselves as a link between poli-

INTELLECTUALS

tics and common-sense. The Bishop of Johannesburg, the Right
Reverend Ambrose Reeves, is one of the most notable of these
clerics. He is a shortish man of wiry and muscular appearance,
who sees affinities between the South Africa of to-day and pre-
revolutionary France, and whose activities are, indeed, obviously illumined by a profound sense of history. Some people believe this remarkable man to be a key figure in the affairs of the
Union, for he is one of the few white men who retain the con-
fidence of African leaders, and he has even established some
working relationship with the more extreme black politicians
thrown into the van by the inanity of the treason trial. He lives
in a big house in the heart of Johannesburg's lavish suburbia, a
symbol of English richness and stability: but I am told that at
moments of crisis groups of Africans are sometimes to be seen
entering his house at dusk, to sit around his study table, brash
and embittered, spouting second-hand Marxist doctrine and
breathing revolution. Bishop Reeves is a Christian, a liberal and
a man of sense, and perhaps after these incongruous discussions
a little of his wisdom sticks, and is carried back in festering minds
and snatches of conversation to the resentful locations beyond
the mine dumps. (And certainly from time to time I fancy I hear
the echo of his opinions in the talk of mining executives and
Chambers of Commerce.)

Even more significant are the protests of the Calvinist pro-
gressives, men like Dr. Ben Marais and Professor B. B. Keet,
whose undaunted nonconformity is among the major political
factors of the day. The straight-jacket of Afrikaner uniformity,
religious and nationalist, is the chief obstacle to political change
in the Union. So long as the average Afrikaner is dominated by
Calvinist dogmas and Boer chauvinism, baaskap apartheid will
ride rampant. Thousands of honest Afrikaners have never even
heard the case against white supremacy and total segregation.
Inculcated at their mothers' knees with notions of racial superiority, divinely ordained hierarchies, fungus, concentration
camps and ox-wagons, they have never experienced the delight
and excitement of new ideas. There is no Opposition newspaper
in Afrikaans. Afrikaner renegades are, all too often, so ostra-

91

cized by their fellows that they move willy-nilly into the English camp: or, if they are men of outstanding character, stay resolutely in the middle, the nucleus of a South African nation. Every day of every week the rank-and-file predikants, the journalists, the politicians, the patriots, the zealots, the Broederbond, and not least the influential Afrikaner housewives, beat away at the old drum of Afrikanerdom. When a dissenting voice is heard from inside the Volk, like the thunder of the ghost in *Don Giovanni*, it rudely shakes the fossilized complacency of the people, and perhaps provides an omen of things to come. There are no more powerful critics of apartheid than Dr. Marais and Professor Keet, both Afrikaners of unimpeachable origins, both devout members of the Dutch Reformed Church.

So, in many fields, intelligence fights bravely against prejudice and intolerance; and it seems to me inconceivable that among so able a community of peoples the old blind bigotries can indefinitely survive. When I was in South Africa a political revue was staged in Cape Town, for the first time in the history of the Union's theatre. It was a riotous success, and when I saw it there were many Afrikaners in the audience, laughing as often as anyone. It was not, by European standards, a very subtle or sophisticated attack upon the established order: but like Dr. Johnson's female sermon, the very fact of its performance was remarkable. For the first time people were actually making public fun of apartheid, of the whole tedious structure of racial theory and rationalization, the never-never Bantu areas, the segregated universities, the pompous dicta of nationalism and biological blarney. (For more than two years an official committee tried to agree upon the meaning of 'race': the most it could achieve was a tentative definition of 'native'.) They laughed at the all-powerful Nationalist ministers. They laughed at the state events of apartheid ('a happy and suspicious occasion'). They even made fun of the sanctities of black and white. It was not very good: but it was new, and gay, and hopeful, and infinitely more spirited than the dreary old credo of apartheid itself.

There are bold opposition newspapers in South Africa. There are impressive numbers of competent and outspoken novelists,

British, Afrikaner and Jewish. There are far-sighted business-men, prepared to defy public opinion to increase their markets or their profit margins. There is a large reading public, one of the most voracious on earth, which is at least subjected, year by year, to the impact of foreign philosophies. The public libraries are splendid, far less parochial and complacent than some of their equivalents in England (you can read the *Manchester Guardian* in Kimberley, but not the *New York Times* in Canter-bury). A growing body of educated opinion stands for change and progress and freshness and adaptability: and I suspect that one day, if only the fates allow time enough, the old barriers will be argued down and the old prejudices scoffed into oblivion. For this is a melting-pot, a crucible, and it ought to be an African Brazil, or an effervescent little America.

11

THE RESERVES

There are black Africans all over the Union, in one state of society or another, but the greatest of the tribal reserves are concentrated in the south-east, where the territories of the Zulus, the Pondos, the Tembas, the Xosas and many another people sprawl like islands of barbarism. When the Afrikaners of the interior speak of the menace of a tribal resurgence, they have their eyes upon these wide reserves, only a few hundred miles away, and their memories on the horrors of the Zulu wars, when the finest black armies ever known fought the white man with such staunch ferocity.

There is a dichotomy in the white South African's mind when he considers the native reserves. In one way he wants to preserve the structures and manners of tribalism, because they ensure that a large proportion of the Union's Africans remain backward, isolated and uncompetitive. In another way he wants to abolish it all, because somewhere at the back of his convoluted mind he feels he has a civilizing mission in Africa, and he believes still in the rightness of the Christian, western way of life. ('The Christian religion', reported a committee appointed to study the country's racial problems, 'is indeed a miraculous power which has radically affected the lives of the Bantu in such a way that no natural scientific explanation can be found for the transformation.') Again, while the conception of independent Bantu areas—the essence of total apartheid—greatly appeals to him in theory, in practice the presence of autonomous black states within the frontiers of the Union would be anathema to him. Finally, there is this primary consideration: that whatever is done for the advancement of the African, however the policies of apartheid develop, the white man needs the black man to provide his labour and sustain his comforts.

The great reserves of the south-east reflect this conflict clearly enough. If you drive through the rolling acres of Zululand, between Durban and Swaziland, you will see the white churches and trim little houses of the missionaries; and here and there you will meet an agreeable and intelligent administrator; and there are excellent roads to take you there, and schools, and a fine hospital at Eshowe; and the office of the mine-recruiting organization is bright and inviting; and outside the trading stores, with their ubiquitous advertisements for Joko Tea and their manner of slatternly benevolence, you will see many a prosperous African in slacks and trilby hat, buying cigarettes or checked socks; and if you give a black man a lift, as he stands forlornly beside the road, he will accept with incredulous thanks —'Wait till I tell them,' he says, 'just wait till I tell them I had a lift from a white man! Baas, you're not from these parts, I can tell it by the shape of your face.'

But sometimes your guide, explaining to you with pride the orderly segregated procession of these reserves, will stop in his tracks, and breathe the splendid country air, and point to an advancing figure with the proprietary satisfaction of a landlord or a cattle breeder. 'There!' he says, beaming. 'There's the *real* Africa, unspoilt, cheerful as a child—can you deny she's happier than your wide boys in the locations? Can you honestly?' And here she comes up the hill before you, waddling slightly and smiling bashfully, like Africa in a pageant, or an attendant at some international trade fair, selling monkey-nuts. She chews upon a sugar cane, occasionally spitting out the fibre, and her hair is piled on her head in a towering structure of mud and grease. A kind of velvet bonnet, like a pin-cushion, is affixed to the front of it, above her narrow forehead. Her bodice is blue, her skirt cream, and she wears a tartan overskirt; and her every extremity, her ankles and her ears, her wrists and her neck and her forearms jingle with bracelets and anklets and bangles and charms. Clanking, gnawing at her cane and sometimes breaking into a high-pitched giggle, this unbeautiful figure shuffles past you and disappears into the store. Your guide smiles. She does smell a bit sort of greasy, he admits, but she's uncorrupted, unharassed, *real*. 'Don't you envy her?' he asks you sympathetically. 'Don't you honestly?'

It is to preserve this pristine innocence, prevent its vulgarization, and at the same time help the African towards a higher Christian society, that the nationalists propose to extend the area of these native reserves and guide them towards complete autonomy. At least, that is the theory. Nobody really believes in it, for the adequate reason that it is nonsense: but the Government spokesmen like to talk about it to visiting journalists, and they distribute maps showing where the new reserves will be, and proving them to have the most rainfall and the best land and most convenient situation and the nicest views of any territories in the Union. The idea is that the present British Protectorates, enclaves within the Union, will be absorbed, and that there will then be established several big Bantu areas, dotted about the northern and eastern parts of the Union. They will not be contiguous. They are practically without resources. To establish them as independent communities, as the visionaries propose, would require immense capital investment, much white skill, and a great deal more fertile land. Within these regions, it is proposed, the African will eventually have full political rights and the white man will have none. Conversely in white areas of the Union the white man will have rights and the African none. This is fine in theory, but ignores the fact that if the country is ever divided in this way there will still be more Africans in the white areas than there are in these never-never Bantu principalities. Most South Africans would probably like a solution along these lines, in their moments of misty principle: but so interlocked are the two societies, black and white, so dependent is one upon the other, so certain is the African that westernization is his proper course, so unwilling are most Europeans to make material sacrifices, that the whole conception of such an idealized apartheid is ludicrously unconvincing.

In the meantime, for all the undeniable efforts of administrators and missionaries to improve conditions in the reserves, most of the Pondos and Tembas and Xosas and Zulus are plunged in ignorance and often plagued with poverty. The great reserve of the Transkei, which bestrides the border between Cape Province and Natal, is crippled by erosion and over-stocking. To most simple Africans a cow is much more than a beast; she is a symbol of wealth and prestige, the price of a wife or the earnest of a marriage contract, and it is desperately difficult to persuade the tribesmen to reduce their herds and save their land. The downlands of the Transkei are therefore brown, arid and crumbly, and they stretch away to the horizon in monotonous disdain. Here and there is a hillock or cliff, from which in ancient times the tribal executioners used to hurl their malefactors or their enemies; and sometimes there are rivers, surrounded by taboos, traditions and ancestral miasmas. Every-where, among their patches of mealie, there stand the neat white houses of the tribal people, round and thatched, built in orderly symmetrical rows like housing estates (or, indeed, locations). A few little towns provide shops, and police, and administration for these wide areas; they are pungently western in style, with hitching-posts, colonnaded stores, and dim-lit teashops in which you may order a tasteless coffee or a rather fatty ham-and-eggs.

This country has a savage past and an intermittently primitive present. Here some of the violent battles of the Kaffir wars were fought, and the coastline—still called the Wild Coast—is instinct with memories of shipwrecks and adventurers. It was in this country that a Portuguese lady was shipwrecked in the 1550s. 'Finding herself stripped naked by savages', say the chronicles blandly, 'she buried herself up to her waist in sand, from which spot she refused to move'—and that was the end of her. The treasure-ship *Grosvenor* ran ashore on this coast in 1782, and people are still looking for her gold. Scores of European castaways, stranded in the Transkei by pirates or weather, are believed to have settled among the tribes, and sometimes you will meet Africans who claim descent from these unfortu-nates: until a few years ago, I was told, there used to be a queer community in these parts called the Mholo, who had black skins but Semitic features, and wore long straight hair down to their waists. Some of the other Transkei inhabitants could scarcely be more African. To this day travellers still sometimes see, shivering on distant exposed ridges, unhappy African boys daubed in white clay for rites of initiation; and it is only a century since the Xosa people, instructed by a false prophetess, slaughtered so many of their own cattle, and thus caused such a needless famine, that in a single year the African population of British Kaffraria fell from 104,000 to 37,000. Battles and slaughters and shipwrecks and witchcraft and tribal dances and chieftaincies and taboos and ancestral laws—these are the stuff of the Transkei and its history. 'The prescribed method of killing a witch', remarks a pleasant little guide-book published by the Round Table in Umtata, 'is gruesome beyond words. A sharpened stick about two feet long is forced into the abdomen per anum.'

One evening a friendly African in the Transkei, home after a contract on the Rand, took me into the country to visit his kraal. We sat in the spotless interior of his mud hut, and chatted rather hopelessly with his wrinkled mother, and played with two or three children, almost totally nude, who wandered in to inspect me. The neighbours, wrapped in ochre blankets, were cold and queer, and looked well able to push sharpened sticks into witches; and in these circumstances I asked my host if he would kindly convey me to a witch-doctor. He did not welcome the idea. Magicians and their kind do not like meddling strangers, and he perhaps suspected that some vindictive spell would shrivel him to the size of a marmoset or turn him into a rock-rabbit. He was very sorry, he said, and he would very much like to oblige me, but there really were no witch-doctors thereabouts, not a single one, and anyway, come to think of it, we ought to be starting for home before it got dark. So we said goodbye to the neighbours and bounced off into the evening in my hired car: but presently, almost without thinking, and more as a joke than a ruse, I sprang a bluff upon him. 'Surely,' said I darkly, pointing to a distant kraal, 'surely there's a wise woman in that village over there? Is there not?' The poor man paled, and shifted most uncomfortably in his seat. 'How you know that, Baas?' he said. 'How you know that wise woman there?' and his eyes widened in dreadful astonishment. 'All right, Baas, I find that wise woman, I find her later tonight, O.K.?'

Sure enough, later in the evening, when the Transkei was dark and silent, that little man came surreptitiously to my side, and whispered hoarsely that the wise woman was outside, already sitting in the car, waiting to foretell my future and give me the benefit of her advice. 'She very clever woman, Baas, very powerful—very much magic!' I peered at her, in the back seat of the car, as I climbed in and drove hastily away from my hotel (innkeepers in South Africa are not very partial to wizardry). She was sitting there all in white, squarish of design and a little frumpish. Her face was high-boned and shifty, but her figure was plump, so that she looked like a well-fed grasping nun. Charms of indeterminate origin and material were suspended from her waist, together with a small collection of bones, and a rather pleasant organic perfume emanated from her person, as if she had been mixing her face-powder with good Devon soil. She was a Xosa, and talked only the peculiar language of that tribe —a tongue so strangely compounded of variegated clicking noises that few Europeans can even pronounce its syllables, let alone translate them—and as we drove she sometimes spoke to my companion out of the darkness, in a cryptic series of clicks, wheezes and expressive grunts. It was as though an artificial being sat behind me, some African Frankenstein, conversing with cathode tubes and thinking in electronics: except that from time to time that wise woman, thoughtfully opening the window, cleared her throat in an unmistakably human way and spat heavily into the breeze.

We drove to a tiny hut, a sort of potting shed, outside which a crippled African woman was squatting over a fire. She welcomed us with respect, and seizing a burning brand lit our way into the shack. It was minute, and very stuffy, and one half of it was occupied by a rough wooden bed. The wise woman promptly lay down; my guide squatted upon the floor; the cripple withdrew; and we were left in darkness. 'She says you lie down with her,' said my guide, so I did. She seemed earthy but almost hygienically clean.

'Clickety-click,' said the wise woman, warm beside me on the bed.

'Give her some money,' said the man.

'How much?' said I.

'Clickety-click,' said the wise woman.

'Two shillings,' said the man.

So squirming uncomfortably on the bed, and getting rather mixed up with the charms and the thigh-bones, I found two shillings in my pocket and pressed it into the eager clasp of my bed-fellow. The divination then began, after the wise woman had performed various preliminary rites, entailing some degree of grunting, murmuring and rattling of bones. A great change was overcoming me, she announced through the interpreter. That was the cause of all my pains, those pains in my head and kidneys, those dizzy spells. My life was going to alter. All the past would be past, and the future future, and my destiny was destined. She could read it all as in a book.

'Listen!' said the man suddenly, in a breathy sort of voice. 'Do you hear that noise, Baas? That's magic people, they want to talk to you!'

I held my breath and listened, but all was silent.

'I can't hear anything?' said I.

'*Can't* you?' said the man.

'No,' said I.

'Not that whistling noise?' said the man.

'Not a thing,' said I.

'Clickety-click,' said the wise woman.

'What's she say?' said I.

'She say magic people want a bottle of brandy.'

'Haven't got one on me.'

'Clickety-click,' said the wise woman.

'Five shillings, then,' said the man.

So I paid again, and hey presto, believe it or not, some faint reedy whistling noises emerged from the darkness, like the first tentative chirpings of young starlings.

THE RESERVES

'Oh, oh,' said my interpreter, 'oh, the magic people's talking about you, Baas. They say you're going to change. You're going to obey those voices in your head, that's what the magic people say. You're going to alter, Baas,' said he, his voice mounting in excitement, 'you're going to change. You're not going to be a black man, Baas, no, you're going to stay white, but you're going to be different, that's what the magic people's saying.' The chirping was now frenzied and incessant, the intervening clicks were ominously loud, and the wise woman seemed to be writhing slightly beside me on the bed. I could hear the man grinding his teeth in expectancy. 'Yes, Baas,' he shouted at last in the darkness, 'yes, that's what they say! You're going to be a witch-doctor, Baas! *A white witch-doctor*! Wheee!'

I thanked that resourceful medium, rolled off the bed, and walked outside into the night: and as we left the cripple hobbled silently from the firelight, knocked carefully on the door of the hut and disappeared like a shadow inside. To such an old woman of the Transkei, the gods of the old Africa are still worth propitiating. The tribe is still more important than the individual or the nation, the spells of magic and witchcraft are still terrible, life is governed by gnarled old instincts and superstitions. For myself, I would not like to have these blanket people for my neighbours, or imagine the witch-doctors as my fellow-citizens, and I would do my best (if I were a South African) to integrate them into the society and civilization of the west: but I sympathize, all the same, with the impracticable idea of insulating them permanently from the white man and allowing them to cherish their own immemorial ways.

And sometimes in my moments of reactionary backsliding, I am tempted to agree with the Afrikaner theory that beneath the most sophisticated black exterior, behind the jazziest and most double-breasted of suits, there beats the resilient tomtom of tribal Africa. An African legend tells the tale of a poor unsuccessful hunter who sat himself down in despair beneath the roots of a banyan tree. At that very moment, so it happened, a neighbouring tribe, recently deprived of its chieftain, was being told by the witch-doctors that a successor would be found sitting beneath a banyan tree in the forest, magically appointed. Out went the elders, found that bedraggled hunter, and acclaimed him their ruler. They stripped him of his threadbare clothes, installed him in a splendid palace, surrounded him with women and riches and foodstuffs, and honoured him with obeisances: but they would be obliged, they said, if he would honour an old tribal convention by never opening a particular door in a corridor of his palace. For years he obeyed this injunction, contenting himself with various forms of opulence and erotic pleasure: but one sad day, overcome by consuming curiosity, sated with yams and salacity, he succumbed to temptation and unlocked the door. When he opened it he found there, sitting beneath a banyan tree, that poor despondent hunter of years before, clad in rags and poverty.

The new emergent Africa, I am sure, will be neither despondent nor bedraggled: but however liberal you are, however kindly and inter-racial, it would be foolish to see only the new-found trappings of the continent, and ignore that little locked door in the corridor.

12

DURBAN

In the middle of these big south-eastern reserves lies the sea-side city of Durban, where the summer is raucous with the holiday-makers of Johannesburg, and the winter is illuminated by the running of the July Handicap, the smartest event in the Union's calendar. When people think of Durban, indeed, they usually think of Zulus, for the city is full of these virile people, and their great black bodies and ornate fineries give an exciting edge to its activities.

This conjunction of the tomtom and the *Tatler* is often piquant. If you sit on the veranda of one of the great hotels, eating a dainty tea and listening to the string quintet behind you, you will be pleasantly surprised to find the Zulu women saunter-ing along the pavement beneath your table, offering their trays of trinkets and souvenirs, gaudy bracelets and ebony elephants, and inviting your custom with dazzling toothy smiles. Up the road from the railway station, where the grand expresses steam in from Jo'burg, the Africans have their market and their beer-hall: a raw-boned, muscular place, where there are handsome black faces everywhere, and courteous manners, and hordes of small boys eating steamy lunches, and piles of wild-cat skins, and heaps of mealie, and hanger upon hanger of loud nylon petticoats, in every shade of orange, red and outrageous pink. There are some famous ju-ju shops in Durban, stocked with extraordinary assemblies of charms and talismans: stocks of old twigs and dried leaves, animal guts, fungi, bundles of bones, strange minerals, jars of powders and rough grey pills. In Dur-ban you can buy hippopotamus fat, which makes you irresis-tible if applied properly; or buffalo's eyelid to rub on your head;

or hyena eyelash, a commodity potent in many ways, I forget exactly how; or crocodile fat, a protection against violent weather; or elephant's liver; or delicate braided tassels, made from the hair of baby monkeys.

And everywhere, a gay link between the cultures, there are the famous rickshaw men, the city's mascots, dragged out mercilessly at the drop of a royal hat, the first clink of a lens-hood or the merest suspicion of a public festivity. They range the streets stylishly looking for custom, from the Coee T. Rooms to the grandiose Town Hall, whistling and shouting and grinning ingratiatingly. Their plumes and feathers wave grandly, their movements are magnificent, but their voices are often incongruously squeaky: and all their rickshaws, I am assured, are made in the United States. ('How marvellously they move,' I once remarked to a lady at my hotel, as two of these massive figures came prancing by, now running gracefully, now leaping easily into the air and tossing the horns of their head-dresses. 'It's rather like how you feel in a dream, when you can fly downstairs, or levitate.' The lady turned and looked at me severely. 'Young man, did you not know that the Astaires themselves came to this city, and saw our rickshaw men, and that's how they got the idea for their celebrated entries and exits, as for example in *Holiday Inn*, which you are probably too young to remember anyway, or *Showboat*? Dreams indeed! They're real enough, young man, believe me!' And as she said this, with scathing sibilance, I noticed the dread gleam of lunacy in her eye.)

For myself, though, Durban remains chiefly a place of the sea. It stands like a grandee upon its bay, surrounded by docks and installations, and the ships sail in past the hotels and make their sirens echo in the hills. The sea, its splendours and its mysteries, are never far away. It was from Durban that the liner *Waratah* sailed one day in 1909 with her 300 passengers, never to be seen again; and when I was in the city research chemists were examining a piece of old metal, washed up on a nearby beach, which people thought might be a relic of that baffling tragedy. Vasco da Gama is said to have sighted the bay of Durban on

DURBAN

Christmas Day, 1497, and named this country Natal: Perestrello charted it in the next century; countless old adventurers, merchants and voyagers landed here for water or trade; and almost every great British warship has put into Durban at one time or another, on her way to Trincomalee or Hong Kong or the forgotten China stations of the British heyday. If you wander along the quay you will find three or four neat little whalers tied up alongside: each morning they sail from this city of pleasure to go a'whaling, returning to Durban in the evening hauling their catch behind them. (During my South African winter they caught a white whale some eighty miles out; it weighed sixty tons and had fiery red eyes, like Moby Dick.) Best of all, Durban is a port for the magnificent packet-boats that bring the mails from England, and play a persistently intrusive part in the affairs of South Africa. In Durban everyone seems to know when the mail-boat is due, just as in the American West any shopkeeper can tell you when to expect the Rocky Mountain Rocket. 'The mail-boat's in,' you hear people say, and at the hotels there are often knots of elderly passengers at the reception desks, fresh from the steamer, cluttered with lap-rugs and golf-clubs, like figures in a pre-war travel poster. One of the great experiences of the Union, to my mind, is to see the mail-boat sail from Durban in the dusk of a winter evening. The gay promenade is lavish with light, its phalanxes of tall buildings ablaze, its strings of fairy lights stretching above the sands, with a glitter of teashops and amusement parks, and the glint of the wheels of rickshaws, and a stream of cars rolling along the corniche, and a distant juke-box, and the whistle of the Jo'burg train. Then, out in the bay, the mail-boat appears beyond the harbour mole, and slides silently away into the night. You can just make out her slim purposeful lines, and the thin stream of vapour from her funnel, above the fuzzy lights of her superstructure; and if you listen very hard, ignoring the cars and the juke-box, you may perhaps hear the smooth unruffled pounding of her engines. For years the mail-boat was the lifeline of South Africa, the only link between this remote outpost and the parent civilization in Europe. To a people surrounded by barbarians, at the tip of an unknown continent, 3,000 miles from a university or a great library or a fine dressmaker or a symphony orchestra or a turkish bath, only the mail-boat brought the promise of support and sympathy. No wonder, when that elegant ship sails nowadays, to vanish so dreamily into the southern ocean, there are often a few South Africans to run across the road and see her go, and wish her a metaphorical *bon voyage*: and if you are susceptible to this kind of thing, the last twinkling of her lights will bring home to you what the Afrikaners mean when they say, in their plaintive moments: 'Man, we've nowhere else to go. This place is all the home we've got!'

Indeed, Durban often feels a long way from Europe. Its façade is a little like Brighton or Atlantic City. Its great occasions are instinct with the snobberies and ill-considered chiffons of Ascot. Cheerful women drive many of its taxis, and bring to the city some slight suggestion of austerity, as though it has just survived the blitz. Hundreds of retired Englishmen live in the comfortable heights that surround the place, and there is a plethora of the usual over-acted Scotsmen. Nevertheless, in Durban you often feel nearer Asia than Europe: and this is scarcely surprising, for so you are. Great fields of sugar-cane surround the city, and the climate is sticky and heavy and semi-tropical, scented with rich exotic flowers, and spattered (if you go to the right place) with the chattering of monkeys and the screams of tropical birds. There are flaming jacarandas, poinsettias, flame-trees, pawpaws, pineapples, mangoes, bananas, oranges and innumerable minor fruits and strange flowers. A third of Durban's population is Indian, imported by the British in the nineteenth century to work the sugar plantations, and these active, acquisitive, litigious people give some parts of the city a sense of constant querulous motion. If you drive to the north, towards Zululand, you will find suburbs so hot and palm-shaded, so crowded with ornate pillared houses, so bright with saris, so thick with thin brown faces and bicycles and mosques and domed temples and incense and gongs, that you might very well be in Madras or Bombay. Gandhi lived here, and launched his first passive resistance campaign in Natal. There are many

highly intelligent Indians in Durban, and many rich ones, and a great number whose commercial instincts are impressively refined and sharpened.

So, of course, there is an Indian problem. There are Indians elsewhere in the Union, though immigration is banned: but most of them live in Natal, and Durban is their capital. None of their neighbours, alas, much like them. The British Natalian finds the beggars too clever by half, and distrusts their competitive abilities. The Afrikaner segregates them, thus forcing their leaders into the camp of the political discontents. The ordinary African loathes them, for he has often felt the lash of their tongues or the extortions of their commerce or the sharp end of their writs of attachment. Most of them have never been to India, and find it difficult to cherish much patriotic pride in Mr. Nehru's achievements. The Indian Government offers to pay passages home for those who want to go, but hardly anybody does; and the South African Indians feel themselves apart from the perennial feud that embitters relations between Cape Town and New Delhi (in one of the Indian airports there used to be a notice forbidding the entry of dogs or South Africans into the dining-room, and a Jo'burg citizen once told me that a prime purpose of the South African Navy was 'to prevent an Indian invasion, of course'). South Africa is a land full of neuroses—the complexes of peoples snatched from their homelands or subjected to diverse alien influences—and the Indians are among the most embittered of all. The Africans cannot yet, in all honesty, claim many citizens of real distinction; but among the Indians of Natal there are a thousand men eminently capable of sharing in the processes of national government, but ineluctably prevented from doing so. They are brown-skinned, and therefore second-class citizens.

The presence of this fertile community in Durban gives the city an extra dimension in racial relations, and the alignments between its various peoples are curious and often complicated. The English-speaking Natalian, by and large, rather likes the Zulu, so long as he is not too westernized. 'He's a decent fellow, the Zulu, as straight as they come. He's a sort of—how can I

107

put it, now?—he's a sort of natural gentleman, you know.' On the other hand, as we have seen, he intensely dislikes the Indians. 'They're a lot of quibbling monkeys, like so many second-rate lawyers—and you should just *see* how they cheat our poor Zulu boys, it really is a shame.' As for the Afrikaner, slowly gaining numbers in Durban: 'The Dutchman? It's like spending your life with a paranoiac unitarian who insists on talking Gaelic. You understand me?'

Many of the Indians are no less contemptuous of the African, as you will observe if you hang around the Indian shops of Durban, and watch the blanket-wrapped primitives sidle in to buy their blazing cottons or their hyena eyelashes. The Indian shopkeeper can be very hard. Other Indians, though, have frankly thrown in their political lot with the black men. Many Indian liberals are active in South Africa, and some of them have appeared at the treason trial in Johannesburg: if ever a concerted, organized resistance movement arises to fight apartheid, the argumentative Indian barrack-room lawyers will no doubt be among its generals.

This is, of course, a direct result of the Nationalist Government's racial attitudes, which cast a stigma upon anyone whose skin is not white, and inevitably throw all these different peoples into each other's arms. When I was in the Union controversy raged about a visiting Japanese seaman who had been discovered drinking a milk shake in a white café. 'We welcome our brothers of Asia', said an Indian broadsheet I was shown, 'and all our brothers who do not share the lily-white skin of the Herrenvolk.' About the same time an African life-saver who had rescued another African and an Indian from drowning was sent £10 by the Government in recognition of his courage: the authorities said regretfully that it would have been £20, one for each life saved, except that unfortunately one of those rescued was an Indian, not a black man. (This reminded me of the Mississippi ferryboats, where some lifebelts are reserved for white passengers only.)

Why, remarked one of the newspapers caustically, that life-saver misjudged the situation—he should have swum straight past the Indian to look for another drowning African. 'He should have considered the problem from an essentially ethnic standpoint.'

This is the kind of nonsense that occurs when a city is forcibly divided into the compartments of racial segregation, and the whole emphasis of social intercourse is on the differences between peoples rather than the similarities. There are, Heaven knows, economic disparities enough in Durban: from the magnificent hillside villas of the Berea, swamped in fragrance and bougainvilia, to the unspeakable black slum of Cato Manor, one of the worst in the Union. But in a more advanced society, less subject to the fallacies of racial theory—in one of the razzle-dazzle states of the American continent, say, there would be a marvellous bubble and fermentation to Durban. It has the assets of a Rio or a Buenos Aires: a glittering seashore, a wonderful country setting, flourishing trade, bold history, vigorous inhabitants, all the promise of prosperity. It ought to be stimulating, adventurous, provocative.

But alas, most of the verve of Durban comes with the ships or the holiday-makers. Suspicion and resentment dampen the effervescence of the place, and occasionally erupt into bloodshed. The fibres of the city are coarsened by mistrust—between black and white and brown, between Briton and Afrikaner and African and Indian. Scarcely an eyebrow was raised, during my visit there, when a native location was raided by the police in the small hours of the morning, and 1,500 Africans were arrested, most of them on niggling petty charges. Bright may be the silks of the July Handicap, and extravagant the coiffures; but some people say that the most inflammable, the most potentially vicious of all the South African cities is Durban, where the rickshaw men glide like dancers past the grand hotels, and the mailboat slips away to sea in majesty.

13

THE FRONTIER

Certainly the bloodiest incident in recent South African history was the protracted Durban race riot of January, 1949, when the Zulus did their best to exterminate the Indians. Some observers argue that the rioters were merely sublimating their resentment against Europeans. Some blame high prices and shady dealings in the Indian stores. Others speak darkly of the African's inherent need to let a little blood now and then, with or without any very rational motive. Whatever the cause, the riots were gruesome: people were burnt alive, and stabbed, and cut in pieces, and mutilated, and only the army was able to restore order.

But this is a country streaked with violence, founded upon bloodshed and the clash of arms. A bond of forceful passions, for example, paradoxically links the Afrikaner and the African, and often seems to establish a strange perverse understanding between the two; sometimes Boer and black man seem to speak the same private language, unintelligible to the Englishman, with a vocabulary of oaths and abuses, and a syntax of bludgeon-blows. The abattoir seems strangely prominent in many South African town. When a nun was killed and mutilated by a mob in East London, many a South African assumed the tragedy to have been arranged by the Nationalist Party, to add point to its racial policies. White South Africans are not, on the whole, squeamish, and take a little skullduggery as a matter of course.

What is more, in South Africa there is still much of the full-blooded robustness of the frontier, and the memory of the Kaffir and Zulu wars is vividly alive. Daring adventure, hazardous expeditions, ruthless money-making, slaughters, executions —all these sinewy masculine matters contribute strongly to the national fabric, and help to harden the Union's sensibilities. The man who discovered the Witwatersrand gold reef ended his life in the north-eastern Transvaal: 'stories circulating in that area', say the guide-books casually, 'say that he was eaten by lions.' Many a South African ancestor was thus gobbled up, or ambushed, or savaged by barbarous kings, or dropped over cliffs, or otherwise forcefully obliterated, and this remains a man's country, where males must be very male, and spend their Sunday mornings fishing for salmon bass in the teeth of blinding gales.

For South Africa is still a young country, and this helps to account for the racial fervours of its peoples. The black Bantu are the Red Indians of the South African frontier, with this difference: there are 400,000 peacable Indians in the United States, but there are 9 million suppressed Bantu in the Union. The historical distrust between the peoples is easily forgotten by the visiting Englishman, to whom often enough a black man is a friendly student in digs at Earls Court, or the Oni of Ife being taken for a ride in the Underground; but many white South Africans think of the African specifically in terms of old wars and possibilities of revenge, and when there is a riot or an epidemic of murders they are all too ready to say: 'You see? They've got murder in their system, they're still fighting their tribal wars.' It does seem true that the primitive instincts of many Africans form a sort of tinder-box, ready to be sparked by politics or injustice, and the threat of these latent passions is never altogether dispelled. The riots in East London and Durban are not the only recent examples. Many a minor holocaust occurs in the locations, without attracting much publicity abroad. Sacrificial rites are still conducted in secluded valleys of Zululand. In Basutoland, one of the British enclaves, there has lately been a spate of ritual murders, in which parts of a man's body must be cut from him while he is still living, and packed into a medicine horn for magical purposes. The terrible crime-rate of the Johannesburg townships, the police raids and endless arrests, even the petty insults and brutalities of everyday life, all contribute to this undercurrent of inherited fear: and there is a direct link between the high-sounding theories of apartheid and the barred windows, the revolvers, the tear gas and the burglar alarms with which the Hillbrow housewife protects herself. In the days when America was afraid of her Indian minorities, the Sioux and the Apaches were perpetual enemies: now that the fear has gone those hard-riding primitives are vicariously honoured, and the villainous Indian chief of the cinema is almost forgotten. If ever a white South African claims proud descent from Chaka the Zulu, as more than one Chicago socialite claims kinship with Pocahontas, the troubles of the Union will be nearly over.

Certainly nobody claims it now, and the social fibre is coarsened by the harsh assumptions of baaskap. There are often suggestions of sadism to the Afrikaner character, or at least a willingness to condone bullying and brutality. Everyone knows that the police sometimes torture recalcitrant Africans, and corporal punishment for adults is commonplace. On one famous occasion a minister of the Crown appeared in Parliament brandishing a cat-o'-nine-tails. In 1940, 1,864 people were flogged; In 1955 the figure was 14,379 (a total, as the newspapers pedantically reported, of 78,573 strokes). The sjambock, the leather whip of the Afrikaner farmer, is one of the symbols of South Africa, and might well appear upon the national emblem, rampant. The newspaper headlines are full of it. People are always being sjambocked, or threatening to sjambock somebody else, and the overseer who follows his convict labourers through the fields of the Transvaal carries a sjambock in his hand, to flick the flies away. 'I'll sjambock the feller!' is what the irate parent says in South Africa, when a coloured man or a liberal makes love to his daughter.

Of course the existing relationship between black and white—historical causes apart—makes for a blunting of sensitivity. To many South Africans the Bantu is little more than a beast of labour, or a commodity, shipped into the mines or farms as you might buy a horse at the county show, or order a winch from Germany. Half close your eyes as the next work truck goes by, and you may begin to see them in this light yourself: there they sit on their wooden benches, a dozen slabs of black muscle, dressed only in a few rags, with their faces expressionless and all but indistinguishable and their bodies bouncing loosely up and down in unison with the jolting of the vehicle. The white men ship these fine dray-horses across the country to the mines; they herd them into stables; sometimes they curl their tails and put ribbons in their manes, and show them off to visitors; often they shoe them well, and give them lumps of sugar; and naturally, as practical men of the world, they give them the stick now and then, too, and keep them on a tight unsentimental rein. If you live in a country with ten million helots, the human currency is liable to be devalued.

On the whole the villainies of South Africa are down-to-earth, black-and-white. It is England's kitchen-garden society that produces the subtle poisoners; in South Africa nobody thinks of extracting the cyanide from the mine dumps, and murderers are more inclined to emulate the methods of that wartime soldier who blew up his grandmother with a land mine. When I was in the Union a murder trial took place that well illustrated these earthy traits. An Afrikaner farmer was accused of murdering his wife's lover and trying to murder her, and the evidence included a letter allegedly written by the wife while the husband was actually in the act of sjambocking her, a new twist even for South Africa. 'I hereby admit', said this document, 'that it is my fault that we live unhappily because I imagine that I am in love with Bill Matthee and save all my energies for him.' All kinds of rock-bottom erotica enlivened the course of this trial and made it, for a week or two, one of the national preoccupations. A statement was read to the court, for instance, in which the accused man declared that he intended to tie his wife and her lover together with rawhide thongs, cut off one of the man's ears, and brand them with the words 'gigolo' and (as he succinctly put it) 'something meaning prostitute'. He ambushed the lovers and shot the man, but did not succeed in this ambitious intention. 'You filth!' said the lover, as the husband advanced with his thongs, and was instantly killed with a revolver bullet. Raw and frontier-like was the supplementary evidence, too, sometimes couched in the coarsest of language ('the dirty thing,' is how the wife is alleged to have spoken of her husband)

113

and enlivened by glimpses of the accused man hanging on to the back of a truck, pouncing all unsuspected on the lovers, finding illicit roses among his wife's underwear, brandishing his sjambok and having small stones thrown at him by his wife. A doctor told the court casually that he had given the wife injections to stimulate her sexually, and after a hearing of twenty days the farmer was acquitted. 'I am through with Martha now,' he told the newspaper public, staring at them fixedly from above a black walrus moustache. 'She has been on with men ever since I met her. I have forgiven her, but this is the end.'

Such a display is a rarity, but to this day the spirit of the back-veldt often penetrates the big South African cities and tempers their sophistication. If you loiter long enough beside the Johannesburg railway station, sooner or later you will see a thin-faced Dopper couple walking by, instinct with the austerity of their fundamentalist sect, and looking ferociously disapproving: they are dressed all in black, from flat hat to thick worsted stockings, and they stalk through the temptations of the great city like St. Anthony in his hermitage. Or in some carpeted drawing-room, among the old silver and the high-fidelities, you may be reminded of the intrusive veldt by some old adventure book, *Five Years in an Ox-Wagon* or *With the Flag to Zululand*, signed, with affectionate regards to his brother Tom, by the author.

Here and there you may stumble upon forgotten little war cemeteries: 'For King and Empire, Here Lies a British Soldier', or 'Here is Buried Burgher de Villiers of Nylstroom, who Died Performing His Duty'. Up in the diamond country there are still a few old-style independent diggers, washing out their pans in the muddy waters of the Vaal River, living in decrepit shacks and only occasionally making an ephemeral fortune. South Africa, both Boer and British, is full of the frankness and hospitality of the frontier. Strangers will suddenly confide in you. Politicians, grand businessmen, newspaper editors, stand upon no fancied dignities, but welcome you at once. In a national atmosphere that remains faintly Edwardian (they call a cinema a 'bioscope' in South Africa) you may still recapture some of the free-and-easiness of the pioneers.

Much of it, after all, is still a wild country, a place of vast spaces and infinite horizons. The Karoo is a wilderness of deep shifting colours, and it is splendid to see one of the old ox-wagons of tradition streaming across so masterly a landscape, with a team of a dozen animals, and a black driver with a long whip, and a wobbly creaking of big wooden wheels. From the railways, too, emanates a sense of space. The trains are not generally impressive, and since they run on a narrow gauge they can never go more than fifty-five miles an hour: but the railway lines remain the chief arteries of the country, triumphantly crossing these huge expanses, climbing the escarpment of the great plateau, and linking the industrial interior with its distant ports. When the train is due there is a fascinating bustle of life and expectancy at any country railway station: the farmer trundling his milk-churns, the pompous station-master ostentatiously checking his watch, a few lean white folk with their suitcases, and a flurry of billowing, voluminous, fluttering primary colours at the other end of the platform, where the Africans assemble. South Africans talk of their trains with affection: and it is certainly a gay surprise when at the tail of a sinuous clanking goods train, half a mile long, there suddenly appears a single jaunty little passenger wagon, all alone at the end, with a couple of sober white businessmen talking earnestly in the front compartment, and a covey of cheerful Africans, singing and grinning and waving and exchanging badinage, swinging along behind.

There is something very agreeable about these open-air tendencies, these reminders of bold yesterdays. If you are at all fastidious, though, they bring their irritations, too. South Africa is in some ways an extraordinarily slipshod and rickety country. That old bus across the Transkei was anything up to two hours late: not through any mechanical failure or emergency, but simply because it was run in the old style, as between friends. The country trains often proceed in a series of picturesque lurches, infinitely nostalgic for those with memories of the gold rush or the opening of the Rand, but fatal to schedules. The public clocks, as we have already observed, have nearly always stopped. Even the big new Jan Smuts airport in the Transvaal resolutely maintains the shanty-town tradition, for its roof leaks, its floors are dirty, its walls are peeling, its tables are unkempt, it is freezing cold, its service is surly and it is unshakably addicted to the South African habit of providing no sugar-spoons, so that the sugar in its cracked pots is stained with the traces of other people's coffee, just as it was in the brave old days of the Voortrek. South Africans of circular tastes often like to describe themselves as living in *laager*, defying the alien forces that surround them on every side: and there are times, when the train crawls into yet another siding, when the two faces of the church clock are stopped at different times, when the rain drips tinnily into the basin beneath—there are moments when one accepts the force of the metaphor.

But I like the lingering ruggedness of life in the Union, and respond easily enough to its stimulation: and even the dreary antipathies of apartheid have their compensations of excitement, as those frustrated revolutionaries will tell you, sipping their illegal whisky, as they listen for the police cars in Meadowlands.

14

KING, FLAG AND EMPIRE

Natal is, *par excellence*, the home of the English-speaking South African. You may still hear people talking of 'home in Dorset' though they have lived in the Union for three generations; and I once saw an elderly moustachioed citizen, beneath a Homburg hat, pottering sedately past Durban Town Hall with a large Union Jack fluttering from the handlebars of his bicycle. Some of the British are still very British indeed. They subscribe to the *Illustrated London News*. They listen in family ceremonial to the Queen's Christmas broadcasts. They are perturbed about the threat to the public schools. They are distressed to hear that the last British battleship has been discarded. Their gentlemanly letters to the newspapers read piquantly beside the Afrikaner protests against nude statues, irreligion or the degenerate United Nations. 'Let us lift up our voices and approach the Government and end this disgrace, or we shall be lost to Afrikanerdom,' writes Mr. Jan Pretorium of Potchefstroom: but 'there are undoubtedly deterrents', says Commander Harrington-Smythe, of Grahamstown, 'for that familiar garden pest, the mole' (and a double-barrelled name, as a newspaperman once remarked to me in Pietermaritzburg, 'still gets a curtsy in this country').

Nothing annoys an Afrikaner more than the frequent aloofness of his English neighbours, or the airy-fairy superiority of whose who are *plus royaliste que le roi*: and sometimes, indeed, one does come across some maddening examples of the breed. A shameful number of British South Africans speak no Afrikaans at all, and often a strain of patronizing contempt enters their voices when they talk of the Afrikaner. 'A bit rough, don't you think?' they will say of your old-school ox-wagon man. 'What you might call a monumental Boer' (which, Heaven knows, is often all too true, but perhaps better left unsaid). In Natal they sometimes speak of seceding from the Union and establishing themselves as an independent British dominion, and at such moments they like to wallow in their memories, personal or inherited, of an England long extinct: a dodo, garden-party England, where nobody talked too loud, and there were parasols in the garden, and we used often to visit Sir Henry—Sir Henry— what *was* his name, now? Never mind, I shall remember it later —anyway he had this lovely old house, oh! the smell of the honeysuckle and such gay tennis-parties we used to have. 'Of course, I know it's all changed now, and I could never go back, it would break my heart to see it all so different, socialism, and strikes, and black men with white girls in the streets, they tell me—and all these death duties and so on. But it will always be *home* for me, Mr. Morris—you may be a *little* too young to understand just how I feel—that's Lindley Hall there, above the mantelpiece, painted by Robert—Robert—you know, very famous—but I'll remember later, I always do. . . .'

When the Afrikaner fundamentalist talks of the western way of life, as he occasionally does, he thinks of the devout severities of the Voortrekkers, and President Kruger on his stoep. When the British fundamentalist uses precisely the same phrase, which she does very often, she is thinking of that distant clink of tea-cups and shine of silver, housemasters and hampers and the thud of soft balls from the tennis-courts. An Afrikaner rebel once told me that even within the ranks of the United Party, of which he was a prominent and brilliant member, he still felt himself patronized by his English-speaking colleagues, especially those of the greying-hair-and-carnation variety. 'Have you ever noticed', he asked me once, 'how they even cut their lettuce sandwiches in the shape of a Union Jack?' A British South African motorist once told me that he usually only gave lifts to people if they were wearing club blazers. 'Would you give me one?' I asked him. He looked at my suit and thought for a moment. 'I'd think twice,' he answered with a steely smile.

But these are incomplete generalizations. The chief contribution of the Briton to South African history has not been one of social delicacy, but of forceful and rugged pioneering: a constant pushing, pressing, relentless progress and aggression. Throughout the nineteenth century the British played with the Afrikaners almost as a cat plays with a mouse. The British were determined to unite southern Africa under the Union Jack, so that wherever the Afrikaner moved he found his way blocked and his dogmas disputed. The Cape itself was annexed. English missionaries and colonists poured in. English replaced Dutch as the official language. The first black men were educated, Hottentots were sometimes employed to arrest erring burghers, slaves were freed and their Dutch owners paid inadequate compensation. Kaffirs were appeased rather than slaughtered. A resolute campaign of Anglicization was conducted.

No wonder the Voortrekkers, determined to follow their own instincts, began their journey into the unknown. (They called one place Nylstroom—the source of the Nile. They had gone so far they thought they had reached Egypt.) They wanted to escape both from the British and from the pernicious new doctrines of humanism. It was not so much the freeing of the slaves that distressed them, one Voortrekker woman wrote, 'as their being placed on an equal footing with Christians, contrary to the laws of God, and the natural distinctions of race and colour, so that it was intolerable for any decent Christian to bow down beneath their yoke'. But the pressure of British dynamism, in the noonday of Empire, was irresistible. The little Boer republics of the interior had hardly a hope of survival. Natal was annexed. The Transvaal was subdued, and Swaziland detached from it. The Orange Free State was denied the great Kimberley diamondfield. When they found gold on the Rand, thousands of foreign immigrants poured in, to be encouraged by Rhodes and incited by the inanity of the Jameson Raid. The Boer War resulted, and the concentration camps, the commandos and the ground glass; until at last the Afrikaners, hounded by the forces of imperialism and modernism alike, found themselves a conquered people.

This is the record, coupled with the activities of Milner and his kindergarten, that obsesses the Afrikaner extremists and keeps the fires of their resentment alight. Even Jan Smuts, a friend of England, called it 'a century of wrong'. Nor was this acquisitive energy all political. A marvellous assembly of British adventurers, often allied with colourful Jews, streamed into South Africa and began its exploitation. 'They Did Their Best', says that certificate from the Association of Rand pioneers: and so they did, with boisterous rough-neck vigour, and few holds barred. Ever and again you may see them in faded old photographs, panning for gold or digging for diamonds or crossing rivers or chopping trees or building railways or lounging in the streets of shanty-towns, vivid, tough, confident, always thrusting: with bushy black beards and tall lean figures, smoking their pipes at their work, or encumbered with shovels and sieves and shotguns. The sly but tremendous features of Rhodes himself peer at you from many a board-room and museum; and Abe Bailey's son is the proprietor of *Drum*.

Much of this business acumen and initiative survives and stimulates still further the Afrikaner sense of resentment. Look at the list of gold-mining directors, and you will find that nearly all of them are still English-speaking, whether of British or of Jewish stock. The fanatics of the Volk like to say that Anglo-Jewry runs the country, and to the extent that its skill and know-ledge keeps South Africa prosperous, so it does. 'Hoggenheimer', a sort of composite mine magnate is one of the villains of Afri-kaner mythology, and people talk about 'the Rand lords', the 'Randocrats', rather as the less subtle Communists like to draw our attention to the manipulators of Wall Street. Most of the big banking and trading corporations are still British-controlled. Nearly all South African gold passes through the London market before going to America. British capital is powerful everywhere in the Union, and the offices of the big companies are often uncompromisingly British in style (but leavened by a resilient frontier spirit, a manner of shrewd informality, that is strikingly absent from equivalent institutions in London). You have only to compare Pretoria with Johannesburg to see how much force and vision the British and their friends the Jews have contributed to the South African milieu.

To-day the Afrikaners, rulers of the Union, are hopefully hammering away at these entrenched economic positions. There are one or two big Afrikaner corporations of impressive ability. One is the Volkslas Bank, whose strong nationalist appeal and easy terms are (I am told) stealing customers from the older British banks. Another is a great tobacco company which has paradoxically found an important market among the Africans. The Afrikaner attempt to gain control of the Central Mining Corporation, the great gold-mining concern was one of the prime events of my stay in the Union: the group also controlled one of the largest English-language newspaper chains in Africa, and so intensely interested were ordinary Afrikaners in these transactions, so significant would be an Afrikaner triumph of this magnitude, so glorious a slap in the face for Hoggenheimer, that the whole of Afrikanerdom seemed to be buzzing with financial gossip. (It did not happen: Central Mining remains unreformed, and when I left South Africa the Argus Press was still the most vociferous opponent of Afrikaner nationalism.)

All this is true enough, and perhaps 80 per cent of South African capital remains in British or allied hands. Yet to the stranger the most obvious characteristic of the average British South African, as you may meet him at the club or in the drawing-room, is not vigour or ruthlessness or pride, but impotence. 'They form the most contemptible of all sections of the Union's population,' an astringent self-critic once remarked; and certainly they are often notable nowadays for wishy-washiness, apathy and pallid escapism. Sport is the god of the British South African. (When a celebrated cricketer decided to stand for Parliament, one of the newspapers remarked loftily that 'Springbok captains, like Governors-General, should be above politics.') His vestment is the blazer, decorated with the emblem of his bowling club, or fishing association, or football supporters' league, or sometimes with the fading crest of his regiment. Wherever you look in the British parts of the Union there are the blazers, with the necks of open white shirts tucked outside

121

their lapels, and the letters E.L.L.H.A. (for East London Lacrosse and Hockey Association) gleaming above the beer mugs. There is a touch of mock Tudor to this society, and an insidious suggestion of vintage cars. The wives, who have all too much time on their hands, read voraciously and talk about Nevil Shute and Colin Wilson and sometimes join the Black Sash, in a lady-like sort of way; but the husbands are usually so resolutely masculine, so obsessed with manly outdoor pursuits, that their conversations are congealed with dubbin and cricket-bat oil. Their political party, the United Party, has a sad reputation for oily indecision. 'I sometimes think I prefer the Nats to the U.P.,' I once remarked to a Natalian of the old school, the King and Empire kind. 'Of course you do,' he replied unexpectedly, 'just as you prefer a Hitler to a Von Papen!' At this moment of their history the British South Africans fall uncomfortably between successive pairs of stools—between apartheid and integration, between loyalty to Britain and South African citizenship, between boldness and tradition. They have no burning conviction to sustain them; and when they want to express their discontent they have no symbol to flaunt (except those brazen irrepressible Jingoes who wave the Union Jack and threaten secession).

I sympathize with many of these weaknesses, distressing though they are to observe (they say this is the only large British community in the world that is not master in its own country). The British South African suffers for his virtues. He has no unyielding nationalist fanaticism, so he is unable to fight the Afrikaner with his own weapons. He finds it difficult to be proud of his country in its present ignominy, so he has no prop of patriotic pride. Somewhere at the back of his mind there usually flickers a gleam of liberalism, so that by and large he finds it difficult to subscribe whole-heartedly to the idea of apartheid, let alone the crudities of baaskap. I once called upon an English sugar farmer at Natal, picking his home at random from the roadside signs, to ask his opinion on the racial situation. He had lived in South Africa all his life, and had established his plantation on an ex-service grant. It was a spanking little place, with pleasant lawns and a smart Mercedes pick-up, but the planter was already having labour troubles. His workers were often lazy nowadays, often uppish and sometimes downright bloody-minded. The agitators had been working on them, he said. It wasn't at all like the old days. 'But you know, though I'd love to give them a good hiding sometimes, you can't really do that sort of thing now. And if I start thinking that way, I take another look at my boss-boy. He's been with me from the start, and he's a real gentleman. I'd happily have him as a guest here in this house—and what's more, he'd vote a damn sight more sensibly than a lot of whites I know. Not that I'm advocating'—added that farmer hastily—'not that I'm advocating votes for the natives! The Nats are right there, you know—you people haven't lived with them. You can't go by a chap like my boss-boy, he's an exception!'

But the liberal instinct is somewhere there, and it is only self-protection that restrains it. When the true Afrikaner divides the races one from another, he is thinking not only of himself, but also of his God. The British South African is at once more progressive and more hypocritical. He is often ready to agree that the black man is organically his equal, and entitled to equal opportunities within the limits of his education or culture; but he knows that the advance of the African may mean a decline in his own standards, less opportunities for his children, fewer servants, more expensive labour, perhaps eventually a half-caste society. This is the key to his political impotence. Everywhere else in the world, wherever he has settled, the Englishman has played a leading part in politics. If he stands on the sidelines in contemporary South Africa, it is because the situation there is uniquely awkward for him. If he follows his liberal instincts, he threatens the integrity and prosperity of his own society: if he makes survival his only object, he has to stifle his democratic leanings.

So he compromises, or procrastinates, or plays bowls instead. He is prepared to speak of South Africa as a democracy, when five-sixths of its inhabitants have virtually no rights whatsoever: and it is only when the Nationalists threaten the liberties of white citizens that he murmurs an ineffectual protest. There seems no way out of this disagreeable impasse: but never mind, it is nice to have the commander reassure us that there really are, despite popular fallacies, ways of out-manœuvring the mole.

15

LIBERALS

Still, not a few British South Africans are among the small body of liberals who stand bravely for a common society in the Union, and have done more than anyone to awaken the world to the evils of racial segregation. In the Union, of course, liberalism has a particular meaning. So dominated is every activity by the nightmare problem of race that many of the usual political alignments are capsized, and the accepted political phraseology is often invalid. A high Tory, rabid for gunboats and prestige, can easily be a liberal in South Africa—provided he believes only in racial equality. He will find himself with some queer allies, Communists and black nationalists and quarrelsome lawyers and muzzy-headed journalists, but he will soon learn to swallow his revulsion. The racial dilemma is so overwhelmingly important that other political prejudices are easily stifled.

The liberals must run the risk of social oblivion, too, especially if they are Afrikaners. Their views are not popular in South Africa, and among the extremists indeed are sometimes considered treasonable, immoral or even blasphemous. 'Liberalist' is a term of abuse, as it was in McCarthy's America; and 'Kafferboetie' means to the Afrikaner just what 'nigger-lover' meant to the hotheads of Governor Faubus's Little Rock. Every sort of accusation is hurled at the liberals. They are agitators, *agents provocateurs*, hypocrites, lackeys of foreign powers, enemies of Afrikanerdom, Holy Joes, suckers, publicity-seekers, misguided idealists, homosexuals, intellectuals, clowns, traitors, Kafferboeties. The little Liberal Party, which indeed has no great chance of achieving power during the next few decades, is attacked by both the Nationalists and the United Party because

125

of the dangers of the split vote; and though its most prominent members are highly respected (for they are often people of great intellectual distinction) their party is a popular object of scorn and ribaldry.

There are some aspects of South African liberalism that I myself find unattractive. I find it difficult to admire photographs of high church clergymen posed in attitudes of devotion. I tire easily of the saintly black heroes of the liberal novels, and the African archaisms in which they so often express their aspirations. There is often a holier-than-thou flavour to it all, an unctuous disregard for normal human frailties, that I personally find hard to stomach. And oh, the agony of the inter-racial parties, when you must listen starry-eyed to some indescribably boring tale of discrimination from a nasty Zulu Marxist; and your African friend from *Drum* winks at you in uneasy embarrassment and wishes he could go home; and, with a swish of heavy satin and a tinkle of bangles, your earnest hostess presses towards you, leading by the hand some gangling African youth, and your heart sinks again as you hear her rich declamation: 'Mr. Morris, I want you to meet William Bingbolugno, one of our most promising young men—now, William, do tell him about that most unpleasant experience you had at the railway station!'—and so you are stuck with him, and he turns out to be, as you suspected from the beginning, an insufferable bore. The thesis that the under-dog is necessarily right is carved deep into the South African liberal mind: if you are feeling mischievous you can always remind them that only fifty years ago, when the Jingoes were burning the *Manchester Guardian* on the Stock Exchange, it was a poor misused Boer, an oppressed Voortrekker, who would be dragged towards you by the determined hand of such a progressive jingling hostess.

Nor do I think the liberals have yet made any great positive contribution to the solution of South Africa's problems, brilliantly though they have exposed its cruelties. 'Apartheid is wicked,' they say, clasping your hand with both of theirs, '—is wicked is wicked is wicked!' This, though very likely true, constitutes a rather nebulous political manifesto, but attempts to

supplement it are not always very convincing. Some liberals
stand for an immediate universal franchise among all the peoples
of the Union, black, white and brown. My wise woman would
be enfranchised, and take her brandy and her mumbo-jumbo to
the polling booths: so would that shuffling charmer with the
sugar cane, and the rough-necks of the locations, and the gum-
boot dancers, and hundreds of thousands of semi-naked pagans
squatting beside their mealie-beds in the Transkei. 'Well,' they
say, 'it couldn't be worse than it is now, could it? Who's a
better democrat, anyway, a rabid Afrikaner nationalist or a
Pondo chieftain? You should talk, look who's got the vote in
England!'

You may perhaps diffidently suggest that universal black
franchise would necessarily lead to black government. 'Oh, no,
no, no. If they did all get the vote they wouldn't all vote for
African candidates. Why, Bingbolugno was saying only the
other day, he said, "Mrs. Spreadbury, if we had the vote we
would vote for the best candidate, irrespective of race or religion." No, Mr. Morris, you've been reading too much government propaganda, this isn't Black—er, African nationalism yet.'
And anyway, she would probably add grimly, she wouldn't
mind living under an African Government. 'What difference
would it make? They would definitely employ white advisers—
it would be only common-sense—and the African National Congress has said time and time again that it definitely has no wish
to drive the white man out of Africa. Oh, Mr. Xobo, how lovely
to see you, *do* come and meet our guest from England—he's
been picking up some very queer ideas—we must put him to
rights, mustn't we?'

This attitude seems to me neither practical nor enlightened,
for it totally ignores the overwhelming opinion of white South
Africa, and disregards the fact that were it not for European
skill, courage and labour the Union simply would not exist. At
the moment (and, of course, the balance will shift in time) nearly
everything that is admirable in South Africa is the product of
white abilities. Short of some mass apotheosis to sainthood, I can
see no reason at all why the Europeans of South Africa should

admit all the Africans to political equality. Most white people feel, and I agree with them, that it would lead to a loss of efficiency and an even further weakening of integrity. They believe the whole flavour of the country would be altered, and much of the work of their forefathers undone. They think it would lead eventually to inter-breeding, an idea which they, like my grand-mother, abhor. They are afraid it might result in some of the horrors of reconstruction and black revenge. Very often their instincts, their upbringing and their religion all teach them that there must be discrimination between the races (the constitution of the old Transvaal Republic said flatly: 'There shall be no Equality in Church or State'). Much of this is nonsensical, much of it self-delusory, some of it's double-faced: but there, three million people believe in it, and you cannot dismiss so powerful and often sincere a volume of opinion simply because it is wrong-headed. These are prejudices and frailties that most of us would share, if we happened to be South Africans; but the extreme liberal solution is a Christian conception of such nobility as to be beyond the ordinary sinner's aspirations.

The liberals are often accused, too, of creating trouble in South Africa by the very fervour of their convictions. They have acted heroically in drawing the attention of the world to the degradations of baaskap and white supremacy, phenomena which (whatever your political convictions) you can hardly con-done. But sometimes, by imputing the basest possible motive to every government action, they have perhaps been misleading. I have no doubt that the aims of apartheid were behind the com-pulsory removal of African tenants from Sophiatown to the new locations at Meadowlands: but I am equally sure that most of those removed are much better off to-day, and that the opposi-tion foreseen by the liberal spokesmen was largely engendered by the liberals themselves. Not everything is criminal in Nation-alist policy. There is a certain grandeur to the idea of total apartheid, and to the vision of the black man working out his own destiny at last, uncorrupted by the diversions and exploita-tions of the west. It may be dotty, but it is not necessarily wicked. You may not mind the thought of your daughter marrying an African, or even marrying one yourself: but put the proposition to your old-fashioned neighbour, to the butcher's wife or the vicar or your Aunt Emily, and you will soon hear, among the green freedoms of England, the authentic voice of discrimination.

So racial liberalism in South Africa, like ordinary liberalism elsewhere, is often characterized by a certain flabbiness and sponginess of thought. It stands indisputably on the side of morality, but it is often as intolerant as its opponents, and much less realistic. It is weakened by a suggestion of priggishness, and by an obstinate tendency to preach and dogmatize. 'We intend to get right down to the hurly-burly, the rough-and-tumble, the wrestling-ring of practical politics,' say the liberals earnestly; but it does not ring true. Perhaps they are too good for the likes of us. Perhaps we feel that, the world being what it is, a little iron, a trace of ruthlessness, a faint hint of temptation is a good thing in a politician. Whatever the reason, we do not vote for them, and we dread those inter-racial gatherings as a schoolboy dreads the arrival of a gushing godmother.

What is more, by demanding equal rights for all, the liberals (and Communists) have induced their African protégés to demand no less. A few years ago the African nationalists were content to ask for a limited share in the government of their country. Now they have learnt to insist upon complete parity. The idea of progressive multi-racialism has been discredited among most African politicians: not because it is unfair or impracticable, but because of the furore of liberal opposition to it. This seems to me a mark of irresponsibility. If ever a revolution occurs in South Africa, it will be partly because the black man has been refused his obvious rights: and partly because he has been educated to a distrust of compromise.

This is one side of the liberal coin: but there is another. Another class of South African liberal opposes apartheid with a harder head and a more universal tolerance. He fights it not because it is always wicked, but because it is patently nonsensical. Such men certainly detest the wrongs of segregation and white supremacy, but their purposes possess a reassuring element of self-interest. Every day of white supremacy, they argue, fans the flame of revolution more hotly. 'I believe in white leadership', they will tell you, 'and I want my children to lead a decent kind of life, in my kind of country. Very well, then, make friends with the Africans, don't antagonize them. Exploit the inevitable. Integrate. Accept the best of them as your partners.' Most of these people advocate some kind of limited franchise, a progressive acceptance of the African into the Union's political life which will preserve white rule until the two races are equally advanced. They believe in differentiation not between colours, but between cultures. They think the African is necessarily moving towards the culture of the west, and that when an individual enters western society he should be entitled to its privileges. In short, they really believe in some system of *évolués*, such as that under which the French, with a degree of hypocrisy, allow Africans to achieve full citizenship by proving themselves educated and responsible. ('Favouritism is the secret of success,' as Lord Fisher used to say.)

This approach bestows a different function upon liberalism in South Africa. In some situations, it appears to me, the first duty of the radical is to foster opposition to tyranny or injustice. This the South African liberals have done with remarkable success, for they have mobilized the whole world against apartheid, and have given some sense of hope and friendship to the African leaders. But sometimes a no less important duty is to guide and restrain the demands of the oppressed. In South Africa, only the liberals can do this. They alone have sensible, man-to-man contacts with African leaders, and can perhaps still exert some influence upon African thought. It seems to me just possible that, helped by the pressure of outside opinion, by the force of economics, by the growing strength of African nationalism, they can synthesize legitimate African demands with the emergence of a new outlook among the whites. They say that in South Africa the struggle will be won by the party that keeps its sense of humour longest: and here the best of the liberals are at an advantage, for they are a witty lot.

Since they are, on the whole, the salt of the South African

130

earth, let me take you to dinner with one of them. He is an Afrikaner of distinguished origins, and he lives in a tall, eighteenth-century house in an old market town in the Cape. He is tall and tweedy, with a thin aristocratic face, and he sprawls among his books convivially, a sherry in his hand, a blossom in his buttonhole. He is completely bilingual, as astute in English as he is in Afrikaans. He is a warm admirer of Hofmeyer, a reserved disciple of Smuts. He believes that if his own policies are best for South Africa, total apartheid is perhaps second-best, with the United Party's attitudes of *laissez-faire* a wretched third. His library is scholarly and eclectic—an almost complete collection of the Afrikaans poets, Daphne du Maurier's latest, Gibbon in a handsome well-used edition, one or two tattered children's books, a huge old family Bible, most of the English classics. He likes rugby football. He disapproves of Colonel Nasser. His dinner guests range from a whole-hog Afrikaner nationalist, greeted by his Christian name, to a gentle Catholic priest and an undergraduate. His wife is stoutish, bespectacled and talkative, and his food is in the Afrikaner tradition: great bowls of steaming stew, haunches of meat, vegetables rich, hot and nourishing. His wine is South African. His cigars are Havana. He talks till midnight, and then tells his son to get the car out and drive you back to Cape Town. 'All right, Dad,' says the son, 'I'll take a sleeping-bag and stay the night.'

His is liberalism of a noble kind: strong, generous, sensible, sometimes caustic. There was a time, in the brief honeymoon that followed the Declaration of Westminster, when this climate of thought might have triumphed in South Africa, when the brave 'twin-stream' Afrikaners were not yet swamped by phrenetic nationalism. Even now such people are not difficult to find, and it is one of the tragedies of the Union that such a reservoir of talent and leadership lies all untapped. What a government they would make, what an inspiration for Africa, what splendid emissaries for the West! Bear them in mind, when Mr. Bingbolugno bares his teeth at you, or Mrs. Spreadbury clasps you warily to her bosom.

16

TEST CASE

The most actively political African community in the whole of the Union is to be found at Port Elizabeth, in Cape Province. I once met some African adherents of a sect claiming physical immortality for its members. Its leader claimed to be 'the Holy Ghost in the Third Person', and also the Voice at Midnight that gave warning to the foolish virgins; and he had assured his disciples that if they believed in him they would literally never die. What would happen, I asked them, if one sad day they woke up and discovered that their prophet had himself expired? They paused for a moment's anxious thought. 'Ah,' they said judiciously at last, 'ah, now that would be a *test case!*' In the political brotherhood of black South Africa, the people of New Brighton, the African location of Port Elizabeth, provide such a criterion: if they cannot achieve emancipation, nobody can.

'P.E.,' as the place is familiarly known, is a prosperous, predominantly English port about half-way between Durban and the Cape. Some people say it is the most heavily prejudiced city in the whole of the Union. Certainly, despite its antecedents, it has readily complied with many of Dr. Verwoerd's desires, and I found it rather a heavy, lumpish, complacent kind of place. Its industries are booming, and on the edge of the town there gleam the chimneys of several car assembly plants, British and American: but its people, by and large, look a froward lot, thin-faced and stooping, like Kentucky highlanders. 'P.E.' has a famous snake park, and a monument commemorating the horses of the Boer War, and a nice club that is inclined (so they say) to black-ball Jewish applicants for membership, and a long stretch of fine sandy beach on which, during my windy winter evenings

132

there, you might observe at statuesque intervals, shivering but rigid in the shortest of shorts, indefatigable sportsmen doing their Sunday fishing. Port Elizabeth is mercantile, inartistic, comfortable, blessed with fine parks and tennis-courts and the most remarkable collection of serpents in the southern hemisphere.

It is also a breeding place of African nationalism. Within the city proper there is a handful of white liberals. One of the newspapers is unique in South Africa in that it does not specify the race of an African involved in an accident or a crime (it was once nearly involved in a libel action when it inadvertently described a white woman as being the friend of an African girl, something very upsetting to Port Elizabeth values). But more important, the location of New Brighton, beyond the assembly plants, is unusually coherent, cohesive and well-organized, and is thus qualified to act as an advance guard of African campaigning. It is a well-planned location, with pleasant small houses and homely garden gates, infinitely more human than the new townships of the Rand. Nurtured under the old tolerance of the Cape, some of its families have had generations of political experience, and they are nearly all Xosas, united by a common tribal loyalty. The location is compact, relatively prosperous, homogeneous. It could well be the core of a South African revolution, the *cadre* of a rebellion, if ever resentment curdled into bloodshed.

In the meantime, it is sometimes a testing ground for other kinds of African resistance. When I was there, they were launching an economic boycott which they hoped might be a model for a national movement. This idea sprang, paradoxically, out of Afrikaner chauvinism. One of the nationalist movements published a list of manufacturers who could be accepted as *ware Afrikaner*—true Afrikaners, and worthy of the custom of the Volk. Afrikanerdom, it suggested, should patronize its own business firms, not those dominated by Jingoes, Jews and Kafferboeties. This propaganda was a mistake. Within a month or two the African National Congress had seized upon so convenient a charge-sheet and announced an African economic boycott of

133

all its products, beginning in New Brighton. More than sixty firms or products were listed, headed by the big Rembrandt tobacco combine, one of the prides of Afrikanerdom. Within the location the boycott was ruthlessly enforced. African shop-keepers were warned with steely courtesy not to buy any more of the banned products, and to rid themselves quickly of stocks they already held. If they failed to obey they could expect no sympathy from their own people. 'It is to be hoped', a circular letter said ominously, 'that businesses affected by this decision will co-operate fully. We trust that no one will invite a boycott of his own business by attempting to break the boycott of nationalist products.'

The campaign was not really a great success, shrewdly though it capitalized the growing importance of African markets to manufacturers in the Union. It did not spread elsewhere, and eventually fizzled out ingloriously. It was curious, all the same, to visit New Brighton during the boycott's early days, and sense some of the hidden organization of the place. The shopkeepers were courteous but cold, and referred me for information to a tall thoughtful African lounging outside: he was the man from Congress, keeping an eye open for blacklegs. I had a letter of introduction to one of the New Brighton politicians, and swiftly and circumspectly was I passed from hand to hand through the location. They did not know who I was, and evidently eyed me with suspicion: but the shopkeepers sent me to the Congress man, and the Congress man referred me to the corner garage, and the garage man put me in the care of a passing clergyman, and the parson handed me over to a fat man in a tight white collar, and the fat man took me courteously to a house with flowered muslin curtains; and the door opened, and there appeared the face of a young woman, graced with a cunning but welcoming smile. She was sorry, she said, my politician was away: but she knew all about me, and that was why I had been conveyed so carefully to her kitchen. It was strange to feel this suggestion of underlying order, and to realize how much can be happening beneath the surface of a location, or behind a white man's back.

TEST CASE

To be sure, it is not often that you come across the shadow of self-discipline in the South African locations. Too often the black people are divided by tribal rivalries, as in the Johannesburg townships, or so riddled with crime and desperation and squalor that they seem incapable of corporate action. Nobody seems to know whether there is any real national underground organization, or whether the African National Congress is now only a front, or whether indeed public opinion is not ahead of its leaders (who are, after all, the unfortunates who stand to get five years and the cat-o'-nine-tails for subversion). Two or three years ago, I am told, most Europeans in the Union were still ready to scoff at the idea of African organization. 'It's the Communists or those meddling liberals,' they would say when some minor demonstration seemed distinguished by the touch of leadership. 'You think the Kaffir could do it by himself?' Now they are not so sure. The bus boycott at Johannesburg was most skilfully organized, apparently by Africans, and when at last a solution was reached, it was by negotiation with black leaders around a shamefaced table. This new African power to force negotiations, still only in embryo, will eventually place the black-white dispute on an altogether new level—a level of putative equality: and some people see in it the most hopeful sign in contemporary South African affairs. (But alas, the African delegates at Johannesburg talked in the sad jargon of Communism.)

I often asked my African acquaintances how highly organized the underground was, how extremist were its views, whether its leaders were Communists or merely nationalists, whether they were anti-white or merely anti-discrimination. But it is queer and rather frightening how astutely the African can shield himself against the inquisitive European. He is not rude or even brusque, and he does not withdraw into an aloof shell like that Afrikaner woman at Bloemfontein. Somehow, though, with an easy, sliding, sideways mental motion he manages to change the subject. A slight flicker of caution or reserve crosses his face, and the glimmer of a smile: and then he is across the ditch, and your conversation runs away down the easy straight of pleasantries. There is a common cry in South Africa, among white people of

135

all persuasions: 'We don't understand the black man, we don't know what's going on in his mind!' In many cases this is because the speaker has never visited a location, never spoken to an African except in terms of the master-servant relationship: there are thousands of Johannesburg citizens who have never seen Meadowlands, and Miss Freya Stark's 'universal sisterhood of women' certainly does not bind within its blithe sorority the South African housewife and her maidservant. But it is not only apathy or tradition that prevents a closer understanding. I did my best to master African viewpoints during my stay in South Africa: but time and again I felt that some impassable chasm divided black from white, and not even the kindly courtesy of the African could bridge it for me. The black man feels this, too. One of the most intelligent and moderate Africans I met in the Union told me he never talked to a European without suspecting the sincerity of the white man's motives, so deep-grained is the racial conflict in South Africa, and so profound the African metaphysical inheritance.

Few Europeans stand astride this divide. There are many, of course, who enjoy happy relations with Africans, especially those who work among the simple people of the reserves, and those with a gift for decent household management. Only a handful, though, can without self-consciousness share the confidences of educated, politically-minded Africans. Perhaps it is not surprising that the most remarkable of all these men (peace-makers or agitators, according to your prejudices) should live within reach of the New Brighton intelligentsia. Sooner or later nearly every foreign inquirer finds his way to Christopher Gell of Port Elizabeth, for Gell probably knows more than anyone about the strength and weaknesses of African defiance. His articles appear all over the world, and within South Africa his name is almost legendary. To his stuffier Port Elizabeth neighbours, he is a fanatic and a freak. To many Africans he is magic. To the reporters and commentators of the world, he is a unique source of guidance and information. To the Nationalists he is anathema. His telephones are tapped, his visitors observed, his mocking trenchant opinions no doubt preserved in the vaults of

136

TEST CASE

Afrikanerdom. He is one of the symbolic figures of the South
African tragedy, exerting from this dull provincial port a peculiar and incalculable influence upon the national affairs. And all
this is the more interesting because, as it happens, Gell is
crippled by polio-myelitis and lives in an iron lung.

Gell is an English-born South African of a truly inspiring
force of character. I disagree with much of what he says; I find
him often intolerant and sometimes unfair; but I have never met
a man I would more willingly follow into the inferno. His father
was a British naval officer, and Gell himself is a former member
of the Indian Civil Service. He talks in the racy, sometimes ex-
pletive idiom of the English gentleman, and nobody could accuse
him for a moment of any fuddy-duddy muddle-headed liberalism. He knows exactly where he stands, and so does everyone
else. 'Don't ring off!' he says, when you telephone and introduce
yourself. 'Wait till I put my telephone down and then listen,
and you'll hear a kind of click when these stiffs stop tapping the
line. Ready? O.K., I'll ring off now—you listen!' And sure
enough, when his laughing voice has gone and you have waited
for a moment or two, you may fancy you hear a muffled em-
barrassed click, as some unseen censor, his ears burning, adds
an entry to the Gell dossier.

In such a gay spirit, fortified by a magnificent sense of
humour, Gell cocks a perpetual snook at the authorities and
contributes manfully to his chosen cause—the emancipation of
the African. A well-trodden path leads to his little house (where
his remarkable young wife supports them both with a physio-
therapy practice). Here the African politicians come from New
Brighton, and the editors of the local newspapers, innumerable
visiting investigators, and a stream of people interested in the
African *risorgimento* and anxious to meet this strange Byronic
figure. Gell receives them in his lung or in his bed (he can leave
the machine for three hours every day). He is very tall, painfully
cadaverous, immensely vivacious. He wears glasses and has one
of his arms suspended above him in a kind of sling. Books and
elaborate filing cabinets line the room. There is a painting of the
battlecruiser *Hood*, one of his father's ships, and the table beside

137

the bed is littered with proofs and pamphlets and letters and open books. Sometimes an African servant wanders in with coffee, carrying a baby slung to her back: Gell treats her with affectionate unsentimentality. Often the telephone rings and Gell, making a grimace at you, launches himself into a torrential farrago of opinion and prejudice and argument, till the voice of the man at the other end sounds breathless and dispirited, and Gell's face is wickedly aglow, and the conversation ends in an intellectual annihilation.

Then, like a swivelling gun or a fire-hose, he turns to you. 'Put that blind down, will you, there's a good chap? Now then, let me put you straight about these bloody Nats. . . .' He talks with tremendous energy, animated, witty, outrageous, caustic, irrepressible, interspersing his diatribes with devastating confidences, pausing sometimes to scribble a name down for you or dash off a letter of introduction, swearing, laughing, quoting Schweitzer, in a most extraordinary flood of stimulation and conviction. Slowly, though, his damaged physique runs down. His breathing becomes heavier and more difficult, his conversation more gasping and spasmodic, his face more strained with effort, and the gusto drains from his body before your eyes, like the symbolisms of a Gothic painting: until at last his wife comes cheerfully in and moves him back to his iron lung. He will still be talking as you leave him, and his anxious humorous eyes will be looking at you in the little mirror above his head. 'Of *course* we're intolerant, James,' he says, as you go. 'We have to be. We'd never get anywhere with these stiffs if we weren't!'

Some people believe Christopher Gell to be a saint. Certainly his presence at Port Elizabeth gives it, to my mind, a strong lead over the Voice at Midnight in the immortality stakes.

17

AT STELLENBOSCH

It is a popular fallacy that the racial situation in South Africa can be adequately summed up in the single word 'apartheid'. Nothing could be further from the truth. Every nuance, every shade of colour prejudice and policy can be found in the Union, from the highfalutin at one end of the spectrum to the bestial at the other. There are those who sincerely believe in the high morality of 'separateness'; there are those who frankly intend to remain boss; there are those who, by a subtle process of double-think, sublimate their coarser motives into something infinitely more pious. It is true that the very conception of separate development, with its concomitants of compulsory movement and restriction, presupposes that power must remain indefinitely in white hands: and, as the United States Supreme Court once decided, in theory anyway the thesis 'separate but equal' itself denies equality. But many South Africans genuinely do not agree, and there are even men of liberal instincts who suffer from the intermittent suspicion that total apartheid may be right.

The fountain-head of higher thought on segregation is the university of Stellenbosch, in the Cape, where the Government has established the South African Bureau of Racial Affairs (S.A.B.R.A.) in an attempt, so the critics say, to rationalize its intentions. Stellenbosch is a gentle triumph of the old Cape Dutch architecture, a serene and lovely style. It is a small town of broad streets and handsome eighteenth-century houses, a white and dappled place, dignified by avenues of enormous oaks. There is a wide green square with a quaint little church in it, and many fine gabled homesteads, and a sense of antique well-

AT STELLENBOSCH

being. It stands in the heart of a lavish fruit and wine country, and not even its Calvinist affinities can deprive Stellenbosch of an agreeable suggestion of gourmandcy (but there I am biased, for in one of its tall terrace houses I enjoyed some of the best food I ate in South Africa).

In this delightful setting S.A.B.R.A. considers its arguments and disseminates its theories. Its influence, or at least its field of action, is wide. I once met a young man at a conference in Ibadan, Nigeria, who told me he had been sent there by S.A.B.R.A. to present the case for apartheid (and a harsh duty it seemed, in a country almost exclusively black and aching for an argument). Innumerable and sometimes lavish are the pamphlets inspired by this institution, and the walls of its building flutter with explanatory maps and charts, demonstrating ethnic truths, Bantu reservations, socio-economic developments or the rainfall of Zululand. S.A.B.R.A. even has its own vocabulary. The very word Bantu irritates the educated African ('Flora, fauna and Bantu,' is a familiar wry witticism) but successfully expresses S.A.B.R.A.'s vision of a people ineradicably different and separate from the Europeans. There is something rather creepy about such an intellectual body deliberately working, night and day, to divide two segments of a country's population and erect between them an insuperable barrier of law and opinion. For it is with the advice of this group of thinkers that, month by month, the Government proceeds with schemes that seem, by any other standards, positively demented: the re-settlement of hundreds of thousands of people simply because they are black, the forbidding of mixed assemblies, legislation on mixed marriages, restrictions on African servants in European houses—the whole nightmare device of apartheid, purposely designed to split a nation in half.

But the wise men of S.A.B.R.A., for all the hostility of world opinion, still believe themselves to be right. A few of them, no doubt, are interested chiefly in hanging on to a good job. Some are guided partly by inherited convictions, religious or social. The rest apparently believe in the solution of total apartheid— the idea of separate, eventually autonomous African states with-

140

in the frontiers of the Union—and if there is anywhere in South Africa where this grandiose concept is allied with a rather frigid goodwill, it is among the racial philosophers of Stellenbosch. I spent a morning with some of them and was treated with great courtesy. Sometimes, indeed, in the course of the morning I thought I detected signs of doubt in their conversation. How were they going to pay for the establishment of the new Bantu areas? Where was the extra land coming from? How would they attract the necessary foreign capital without the radical change of policy demanded by the rest of the world? How would they replace their lost labour? What about the Africans left within European areas—would they have no rights at all? If not, since they were the most educated and articulate of the Union's Africans, would not the political situation remain much the same anyway? They talked about complete autonomy for the Bantu areas, but when was it going to happen?

Once or twice it seemed to me that they wavered. Yes, they said, the provision of capital was a problem. Africans within white areas—well, that was a difficulty, certainly, and it might be that they would have to be given some political rights. A time-table for autonomy—'Yes, Jan, that is a very good idea, I think we should work out a schedule—it's a good idea.' From time to time I thought their assurances were cracking. But no, towards the end of the morning their convictions rose rampant. 'If we send every possible Bantu back to the reserves, then we shall have to make do without our easy black labour. We shall have to be agriculturists again, Mr. Morris, like in the old Boer republics. We shall have to learn to use our hands again, like our forefathers of old, and the Voortrekkers themselves—we shall have to get used to handling muck ourselves. We shall have to mechanize our industries. We shall have no rights in the black areas, and the natives will have no rights in ours. Every Bantu in our European regions will be a visitor or a nomad—if he wants political rights he must stay in his own areas. But think what it will mean for the Bantu, Mr. Morris!' they cried, a dim gleam of some kind of fanaticism entering their eyes. 'They will lead their own lives at last, free to follow

141

their own courses and instincts. No more aping of the white man! No more of these terrible urban slums! Believe me, Mr. Morris, we know as well as you do how horrible some aspects of white supremacy are—don't you see, man, in their own country the Bantu would be free of all these degradations and insults? They would be their own masters again. It's the only way. It will mean sacrifices from us as well as from the natives— separate development is an act of faith. The time has come when we've got to reverse a tendency, and prevent black and white from coalescing. If the two people integrate it will mean tragedy for all of us. So we've got to separate them—just like Germany and Britain had to set about rebuilding themselves after the war. This is a surgical operation, man. We're not just a lot of damn bullies, like you people think we are!'

Nor they are. At this level of thought the concept of complete apartheid, the deliberate sundering of the two racial groups, has a mystical flavour to it. Here the doctrine of ends justifying means is carried almost to lunacy. These gentle dons of Stellenbosch, sipping their coffee and arguing, are defying the whole gigantic movement of world history. They ignore all the shifting balances of power and development, the rise of the black and brown nations to independence and eminence, the decline of Europe, the emergence of the great inter-racial nations like Russia and the United States, the eclipse of the old-school empires, the debunking of old racial theories, the existence of the United Nations, the advent of humanism itself. They are grandly insulated from it all. I can well understand why South Africans do not want the shape and texture of their society altered by the emancipation of Africans: but talking to the lofty theorists of apartheid is rather like having a tutorial with some magnificently unbalanced professor of fiction, an interview with a Baconian cryptologist or an inventor of perpetual motion, or a cosy fireside chat with an old lady who thinks she is a poached egg.

At the other end of the scale, where religious certainty and Afrikaner nationalism trail away into plain baaskap, there is a parallel element of derangement. We have seen already how crude and basic can be the emotions of white supremacy—

AT STELLENBOSCH

simply the determination of the white man to stay on top, come what may: but there are also, in many simple minds, notions of eccentric theory and principle. It is not so easy as you might suppose to detect the Charlestonian outlook—those zealous arguments of the American South that range with such fluency through every shade of medical, historical and ethnical fancy, supported by a diminishing degree of logic every year. Sometimes, though, one does hear the authentic voice of wild-eyed biological racialism. When I was in South Africa, for example, there was a controversy about blood transfusions. Word went round that Africans had been giving blood to hospitals and that if you were involved in an accident you might find black blood being pumped into your veins. To the white supremacy fanatic, this smacked of the horrors of space fiction, so awful was its import. It was useless to argue, as most South Africans did, that the blood-stream was changed every twenty-four hours anyway, so that even if you had Kaffir corpuscles to-day, to-morrow you would be all unsullied again. 'The Almighty will not tolerate this unnatural practice,' thundered the zealots. 'It is flying in the face of nature.' Within a week or two, to pile terror upon terror, a story arrived from France to the effect that a scientist in Paris had discovered a system of changing the pigmentation of skins: black could be made white, and vice versa. This staggering blasphemy silenced even the wildest of the bigots. If black could become white, the end of the world was in sight, and it was useless to protest.

There are a few old diehards who refuse, on obscure Mendelian grounds, to shake hands with an African. Many, of course, prefer not to 'because I don't like the thought of it'—so do many English people. Even more consider it socially or perhaps politically wrong. But now and then you may be told in the Union that contact between black and white skins is 'pigmentorially harmful, because of the interchange between sweat pores and the consequent integration of corpuscles'. Some people, I am told, seriously think the black may come off on to them. Many complain of the smell of the African. 'Kaffirs stink,' they say with a grimace. There is some truth to this—the African does

143

have a distinctive smell, musty and pungent; but much of the smell they complain about is simply the dirt and sweat of poor people, and I have smelt like it myself, very strongly, after a few weeks without baths or beds or civilized comforts. I once observed to a white South African that to African noses the European body had a peculiar odour. This is common knowledge, as even your best African friend will admit; but my companion had never heard the suggestion before, and found it most intriguing. 'Would you credit it, then,' he mused, 'Kaffirs thinking we stink! That's rich, that is!'

Most of us probably share these irrational prejudices to some degree, however resolutely we stifle them. To us the black man is a stranger, a phenomenon from the unknown continent of our grandfathers, a reminder of imperial responsibilities. To the South African he is also a recent enemy and a potential menace. No wonder there are innumerable deep-rooted impulses to be restrained before he can be accepted in the Union as a normal human being. Even people who advocate the integration of the races sometimes have trouble with their intuitions. One earnest liberal told me that he often had Africans to stay with him at his house. 'You know it's an awful thing to admit, but I simply can't bear the thought of them using my lavatory. They sleep in my beds and they eat at my table, but I have to ask them to use the outside lavatory. Shameful I know, but there it is. . . .' A few kindly hostesses dislike Africans in their bathrooms in case they blacken the towels. South African Airways, they tell me, insist that headrests used by African passengers must be washed separately from those used by Europeans: some mysterious essence might be transferred, by way of the linen and the lather, from a black head to a white.

But the most stubbornly undaunted of the cranks are those who justify racial segregation on religious grounds, and who claim that apartheid itself is decreed in holy writ. There are those who point to the scriptural story of Ham, father of all the black Hamites, to prove the divine origins of racial stratification. This particular text rather baffles me, for in fact nothing very terrible seems to have happened to Ham. His son Canaan, it is true, suffered the curse of God, to be 'a servant of servants unto his brethren': but Ham himself was unscathed, and had several other children, Cush, Phut and Mizraim, any one of whom (it seems to me) might have been progenitors of the poor Bantu. 'But he shall be a hewer of wood and a carrier of water,' cry the extremists, 'for he is of the seed of Ham, and cursed be his seed, he shall be a servant of servants in the land (or we shall be swamped, don't you see, man?).' I asked one Afrikaner academic what he thought about the racial dilemma. 'Well, it's sad,' he said, 'but in principle it's simple. You see, you must realize, Mr. Morris, that we are divided into our separate races, black, brown and white, *according to our degree of original sin.*'

An allied school of thought maintains that the African is biologically or spiritually incapable of achieving equality with the European. History proves, runs this argument, that the African has never evolved an organized society, beyond the primitive groupings of tribalism, and has never produced great creative art. If you point to the Benin bronzes the answer is that they were probably made by Portuguese renegades, not by Africans at all. If you instance the Negro notables of the United States, Ralph Bunche or Paul Robeson, they will reply that all such people have an infusion of white blood. If you recall the be-feathered discipline of the Zulu armies, they will answer: 'For war, perhaps, but for peace never.' If you mention Ghana, they will say yes, exactly. Sometimes, in my brooding reactionary moments, I have a skulking suspicion that there may be something in this theory, for all the scoffing of the geneticists. It has recently suffered, though, a telling reverse. For generations the proud ruins of Zimbabwe, just over the frontier in southern Rhodesia, have provided a splendid puzzle for the archaeologists, who have variously attributed them to Arabs, Chinese, Egyptians and even, in their exuberant moments, Romans. Alas for the South African racialists, a new theory is now more generally accepted: this marvellous city was built by Bantu tribes, during a period of advanced and florid civilization.

So the poor South Africans, searching for solutions, argue their case for supremacy. Contain your sympathy, if you (like

145

me) cherish a little. This is a country of miscegenated motives, and often these mad or high-sounding justifications mask more prosaic emotions; self-defence, lust for power, obstinacy, or that streak of plain selfishness that is common, God knows, to us all.

18

GARDEN AFRICA

Stellenbosch stands on the edge of the golden country: the rich
and beautiful hill regions of the western Cape, valleys lush with
vines and tobacco, gentle mauve mountains, spacious punch-
bowls, ornate old farm-houses and benign villages. When the
wanderer thinks of South Africa he remembers as often as not
this delectable place, and he cannot understand it when his
London hostess says apologetically, pouring him a drink:
'Africa! ugh, I'm sorry, but I can't just work up any interest in
that horrible continent.' She is thinking of jungles and deserts
and Mr. Bingbolugno, and she has never seen the serene
majesty of Kilimanjaro, the dazzling Ghana coastline, Zanzibar
or Marakeesh, or this generous garden of the south.

The western Cape is the most tolerant and easy-going of the
South African regions. If you travel there from the Free State
or the Transvaal you will notice instantly a relaxing of tension,
a sense of genial give-and-take, a fading of bigotry. Until a few
years ago the half-caste people of the Cape (the 'Cape Coloureds')
were on a common voters' roll with the Europeans, and to
this day a handful of Africans in Cape Province enjoy voting
rights (they elect the Natives' Representatives who alone represent the liberal cause in the Union Parliament). Natal faces east;
Transvaal and the Free State stand like islands in the interior;
but the Cape is indisputably a western country, nurtured and
cherished by centuries of contact with Europe. When your car
brings you to this pleasant place, out of the wide Karoo or the
reserves, you will take off your tie, perhaps, or throw your hat
in the back seat, or perform some such little act of liberation to
celebrate your crossing of an ill-mapped Rubicon.

147

GARDEN AFRICA

But though the air is freer and softer, and there is a more
recognizably English or European feeling to life, there are communities in the western Cape almost as insulated and introspective as any incorrigible settlement of the Boer platteland. Some
such communities are poor and backward, and live tucked away
in remote mountain valleys, assiduously inter-breeding; others
are prosperous and accessible, and are inhibited only by their
anachronistic sense of values. A remarkable example of the
latter phenomenon is the wine-growing society of the Drakenstein, a valley so delightful and so bountiful that Cecil Rhodes,
in one of his monumental moments of extravagance, lightly
ordered his agent to buy the whole of it. Most of the South
African wines are produced in this part of the province: ries-
lings, burgundies, clarets, and those blushing sherries with
which the more worldly kind of Oxford don likes to lubricate his
reluctant pupils.

The great wine-vats at Paarl, the centre of this region, are the
biggest in the world, though not the most distinguished. Coopers
come from France and Portugal to construct or repair their immense barrels, and the most lavish Swedish, French and Swiss
equipment produces the wine in conditions of hygienic perfection, throwing in one or two by-products like eau-de-Cologne.
I spent a most agreeable morning inspecting this place. We
sampled two or three sherries before our tour began; and paused
in the middle to taste a burgundy; and enjoyed an excellent
bottle of Cape Riesling over lunch at the local inn; and left
Paarl hugging a presentation hamper, containing a bottle of
sherry, a bottle of brandy, and a dainty flask of eau-de-Cologne,
with love from the Wine-Growers' Co-operative. The vines are
descended from European scions—Palomino, Carberne, Riesling, St. Emilion, Tinta Roriz and Pinot—first transplanted at
the end of the seventeenth century. For several generations a
South African dessert wine, Constantia, was one of the honoured
liquors of the world, celebrated in the writings or witticisms of
Sheridan, Jane Austen, Dumas, Baudelaire and Longfellow, not
to speak of countless anonymous *bons viveurs*. Nowadays the
sherries are Paarl's most important products. Just before the
148

war, so I was told, some bright scientist contemplated the fact that Paarl was climatically akin to Jerez de la Frontera, the Spanish sherry country; and this led him to wonder if the Cape vineyards possessed in their soil the rare yeast cell called *flor* which gives Spanish sherry its characteristic qualities. They investigated: and sure enough, say the Paarl publicists, the priceless *flor* was there. Many Spanish vine-growers frankly disbelieve this, and certainly the Union has never produced a really first-class pale dry sherry. Nevertheless, 600,000 gallons of South African sherry leave the Cape each year, *en route* for gullets of undergraduates and men of thrift.

Many of the Drakenstein wine-farmers are of Huguenot descent, and most of their wine is priced and marketed by the Co-operative. This is a paradoxical organization. It is overwhelmingly Afrikaans in language and *mores*, but it is devoted to selling as much alcohol as possible on the widest possible market. I attended its annual meeting, in a big hall at Paarl. There were several hundred wine-farmers there, leathery, austere-looking men, with monotonous voices and stodgy opinions. Dr. Malan's brother was in the chair, and he sat there on the platform looking dark and deaconesque, with six or seven other men of similarly puritanical bearing. There could scarcely be an assembly, you might suppose, more obviously dedicated to every facet of white supremacy. Yet what that meeting was demanding was this: that Government restrictions on the sale of wine to natives should be lifted. 'It is iniquitous,' they said. 'Because the natives cannot buy wholesome liquor legally, they go to the shebeens and drink all manner of evil concoctions. This is a betrayal of our sacred trust! Such wicked liquor rots morals and stomachs alike. It encourages vice and immorality. It leads the Kaffir to haunts of crime and squalor. It is a betrayal of the white man's trust towards the ignorant native!' (And if only Kaffirs could buy our cheap wines, those frowning moralists might have added, how marvellously our markets would be extended!)

Already, thanks largely to dirt-cheap labour, the Cape wine-farmers live in considerable comfort. In their fields the floppyhatted Coloured men work in bent-back rows; and you may often observe a line of convicts, in shirts with scarlet stripes, from the spanking new farm prison down the road. Inside the well-proportioned white farm-houses the farmers and their wives live in a style bordering upon elegance. At some times of the year, when they are crushing the grapes, these houses are a turmoil of work and dirt, and there are visiting labourers sleeping on the stoep, and all the orderly routine of the wine-farm life is thrown, for a few frenzied days, to the winds. But in the mellow glow of a South African winter such homesteads are serenity itself. A well-polished car stands in the garage and two lithe greyhounds, perhaps, gambol on the lawn beneath the big oaks. In the garden at the back a thin layer of autumn leaves loiters upon the surface of the swimming-pool. Your hostess wears crisp English cotton and a cardigan, and puts her fashion magazine in a rack as you approach; and the farmer himself, in well-pressed shorts and an open-necked shirt, strides in from the fields like a Surtees squire from his estate. One family I met had just come back from a little vacation in the Far East, and in the drawing-room there stood an eerie souvenir of their journey: a slab of roof tiling, solidified or fossilized by the atomic explosion at Hiroshima. Did it not constantly remind them, I asked, as it stood there on the mantel-piece, of nuclear horrors and tragedies? 'Mm, yes, it does some-times,' said the farmer, handing me a cup of coffee, 'but don't worry, it isn't radio-active.'

For these prosperous people, like many of their simpler com-patriots, are often able to erect around themselves a stockade of stubborn unreality. They refuse to allow the progress or re-gression of the world to shake the easy equilibrium of their ways. One of the notorieties of the Cape is the 'tot' system, which legally allows the wine-farmer to pay his Coloured labourers partly in cheap sweet wine. I asked if I could see this system in operation and was directed to a farm, low and rambling, set in a delectable gulley in the hills and surrounded by vines and fruit trees. The farmer met me at the gate, a Huguenot with black drooping moustaches and unexpectedly bright bead-like eyes. He wore an old trilby and a long funereal overcoat, and he wel-

comed me to his farm with easy style. 'You're just in time,' he said. 'We give them six tots a day, you see—one when they start, one at breakfast, one at eleven, one at two, one at four and one when they finish work. Let's see, it's five to four now, we've got time for a cup of coffee first.' So we sat comfortably on the stoep, and a servant brought us coffee and we tasted some juicy guavas from his orchards. The sun shone gently over the Drakenstein; one or two obscure southern birds sang in the trees outside; and beyond the vineyards the hills rolled away into a shimmering hazy distance. It was lovely.

But presently we heard throaty voices outside and a patter of bare feet. 'There they are,' said the farmer, 'drink up!' We finished our coffee and I took the opportunity of discarding my guava (a fruit I am not addicted to) behind a neighbouring bramble. We walked to the side of the house, where the cluttered outhouses stood: and hey presto, by the queer magic of South Africa, we found ourselves instantaneously in another world. There stood the labourers in a quivering queue, seven or eight tattered Coloured men, sweating a little. Their faces were vacuous and mazy-looking, and some of them smiled foolishly when the farmer and I approached. On the steps of a nearby barn the white overseer was doling out the tots. He had a big bucket of thick red wine before him, and as the workers came shambling up with their old baked-bean tins, he scooped them their ration in silence. It was an eerie spectacle, for it was perfectly plain to me that those dazed and ravaged half-castes were in a state of perpetual debauchery. Their eyes had the glazed bloodshot look of the incorrigible drunk, and their bodies seemed to be shaky and ill-controlled. Up they loped, one by one, and presented their old tins: and quaffing their tots in one experienced and joyless gulp, they shuffled swiftly away again. It was not a moment for human refreshment, like the gossipy tea break in an English factory: it was more as though eight elderly machines were being greased or refuelled, as prescribed in the instruction book.

'Yes, we give them six tots a day,' said the farmer chattily, 'that's the law. It comes to a bottle and a quarter a day. They sweat it out very quickly, but it gives them kick, you see. It keeps them working. And the calorie content is very high,' he added, sensing perhaps a certain sales-resistance on my part. 'It's a good cheap wine—here, taste it!' And with fastidious courtesy the foreman, producing a tin cup from inside the barn, wiped it carefully with his handkerchief and drew me a ration. 'It's quite all right,' he said kindly, 'nobody's drunk out of this cup.' The wine was heavy, but not disagreeable. 'Some people do say', the farmer observed, as I drank it with caution, 'that it's bad for their health, but I don't know. It's what they want. I'd give them tea or coffee if they wanted it, but they've been doing this so long they've got used to it, see?'

The last of the labourers was an old man in a tumbled hat, with a tangled grey beard and eyes covered with film, like a lizard. As he passed us he grinned at me inanely. 'There!' said the farmer, chuckling genially, 'That old man's been doing this for thirty-five years. Thirty-five years at a bottle a day! He's sozzled all the time, but it's amazing how it gives 'em punch, and keeps 'em working.' As he drank that broken old man deliberately turned his back on us, as though at the back of his fuddled mind he was somehow ashamed of his degradation: and then, leering at us again, he ran shakily away down the path. I watched him go, ungainly and lopsided among the vineyards, until at last he disappeared into the shadows and only the heavy smell of the wine was left lingering around the barn.

This is the prime peculiarity of South Africa: that suddenly you may come across a way of thought, a mode of life, totally immune to the transitions of history. It is like one of the disconcerting time-shifts of space fiction to stumble upon such an islet of anachronism, to feel yourself in an alien age or some shuttered eccentric Shangri-la, as you watch those dissipated labourers stagger back to their work.

'Africa, ugh!' says that opinionated hostess in London, but the visiting South African smiles tolerantly. 'You're thinking of jungles and deserts and Mau Mau,' he says. 'You've never seen Kilimanjaro, or Zanzibar, or our lovely garden valleys of the Cape.'

19

DIAMONDS

Anyway, this is only one aspect of Cape Province. It is a big place, and marches away from the sea to the arid territories that border upon Bechuanaland. Its charm and its pervasive character spring from the south-west, the oldest and kindliest of the South African settlements. Its wealth comes largely from the north, on the frontier of the Orange Free State, where there stands in honoured isolation the celebrated little city of Kimberley. The Rand is the basis of South African power and prosperity: but Kimberley is the basis of the Rand, for its diamonds financed the great gold magnates, bolstered the ebullience of Rhodes and his peers, and enticed the first vivacious flood of adventurers and fortune hunters to South Africa. They find diamonds in many other places, too. They even manufacture them nowadays. The Cullinan, greatest of them all, was discovered in the Transvaal. In South-West Africa they pick them up in handfuls from the beach. In Tanganyika they guard the deposits with radar mechanisms. But Kimberley is the most famous, the most suggestive of all diamond cities, and to the world at large its name remains more or less synonymous with the allure of precious stones.

I love diamonds, and so love Kimberley. It has none of those sinister undercurrents that make the gold cities eerie and foreboding (though Heaven knows the international diamond industry is queer enough). It stands in a hot and disagreeable plain, a dusty smallish town of yellowing buildings. Its shops are rather shabby and its town hall, when I was there, showed every sign of incipient demolition. It is not in short, a sparkling municipality. But the past of Kimberley feels much more potent than its

DIAMONDS

present, and as you wander through these drab but genial streets you feel yourself very close to the rollicking days of the place, when the freebooters roistered the evenings away in its saloons, Cecil Rhodes himself stalked acquisitively among its workings, and Barney Barnato, the most remarkable of them all, juggled with his bowler hat, reminisced about Whitechapel, and amassed his gigantic fortune. Here is the famous gun, Long Cecil, which an American engineer designed and built in the mine workshops during the Boer siege of Kimberley: and here, for that matter, is the hotel in which the same engineer was killed by a retort from the Boer artillery. Everywhere there are reminders of war or of boisterous enterprise, disused workings, the skeletons of trenches, enshrined guns and the conversations of mining men. Kimberley has a faded, haunting frontier magic, and there is nothing more evocative in South Africa than the ill-printed little placards, tucked in cottage windows, that announce to the passer-by: 'Licensed Diamond Buyer Within.'

And in the very centre of it all, surrounded by half-hearted and intermittent shacks and cottages, there plunges the Big Hole, from which the magnates extracted their fortunes and their fame. There was never a more striking memorial to an epoch of history. It does not seem a very wide hole, and a few little shrubs grow domestically around its perimeter: but it is dramatically, ludicrously, frighteningly deep. The Kimberley sky is bright and cheerful, and little specks of mica or other specious minerals sparkle in the dry soil: but if you peer over the edge of the Big Hole you can see it dropping away into the gloom with infinite enigmatic age, a distant dark glitter of water at the bottom and a faint smell of earth and damp. It is extra-ordinary, and unconvincing, to consider that this vast pit was scrabbled into the surface of the earth by men's hands and tools. At the beginning, of course, it was merely a shallow declivity in the ground, and the miners taped off their claims and worked side by side within its boundaries. Then, as each man lowered the surface of his claim, it looked like a huge waffle, intersected by ridges left for the carts that must haul the soil away. Still deeper they went, and the ridges collapsed in despair, and they had to establish an eccentric system of pulleys to haul the muck to the edge of the hole. Each little claim—sometimes only 15 or 20 feet square—was linked by its own winch to the rim of the mine, where the soil was searched for diamonds; so that the entire hole was criss-crossed with thousands of ropes, taut or drooping or bustling, like a mesh of colossal cobwebs. A multitude of speculators worked in this deepening pit (in one year nearly 50,000 hopefuls came to Kimberley), squabbling and intriguing and drinking and loving and sometimes committing suicide, until at last Rhodes and his syndicate bought most of their rivals out, sealing the issue with the most valuable cheque ever signed, upon which you can still see, scrawled in a flowery pedantic script, the rolling incantation: 'Five million three hundred and thirty-eight thousand six hundred and fifty pounds'—to which is added what looks suspiciously like the bathetic afterthought 'Only'.

Many of these thrusting miners were Englishmen, of that classless company, ranging from deserters to bishops' sons, that has helped to open so many of the world's frontiers, from Deadwood Gulch to the Snowy Mountains. There was a time, soon after the discovery of diamonds, when it seemed that Kimberley would enrich the Boer Republic of the Orange Free State. But the British were all-powerful in those days, and the place was skilfully detached and firmly united with the Cape, to the lasting chagrin of Bloemfontein and the Broederbond. To this day it remains resiliently English in form and flavour, a tolerant and friendly city, larger than it feels. There is little tension or antipathy in the air, and your taxi-driver may well confide in you his belief in limited franchise for the natives. In the warm little public library you can read the *Spectator* or the *Listener*, and when I stepped out of its door one day I came face to face with a woman of such transparent Englishness, such comfortable familiarity of bearing and appearance, that our very glances shook hands as we passed each other. You still hear Welsh or North Country accents in Kimberley, and you sometimes notice signs of old English aberrations. In the mine museum there is an antique tricycle, fitted with a large white sail, upon which a

DIAMONDS

Mr. John Derbyshire once journeyed in erratic lurching spasms all the way from the south coast to the diamond diggings. On the walls of my hotel lounge three pictures stared at me with homely fustiness, the very breath of the English provinces: there was 'Dreaming', in which an entirely naked girl leant uncomfortably against an elm tree; and 'Daybreak', in which another dainty nude, full of fun, is awakening a friend upon a classical balcony overlooking a lagoon; and 'Vespers', in which a small child of daunting piety stands lost in prayer among her sheep. 'Here's a funny joke,' a man remarked to me in Kimberley one day. 'The first man says, "Did your father die intestate?" and the second one says, "No, he died in the Free State!" Get it?'

Racially, too, the town is reasonably generous and easy-going. The edges of segregation are blurred and smudged, so that you find little peninsulas of black, unobtrusive archipelagos of white. Miscegenation does not feel a menace or an obsession, though I have no doubt the idea of it sometimes troubles anxious mothers. Africans are not treated altogether as beasts of labour. I was once walking down a street in Kimberley when I heard the sound of cheerful chanting from an alley-way. I walked around the corner, and found a gang of black labourers stamping down the surface of the pavement after some plumbing operation. They heaved and hammered and swung their implements in an easy rhythm, and sang this bright monotonous song as they did so. 'What's it mean?' I asked their white overseer. He pushed his hat to the back of his head and looked thoughtful. 'Bert,' he said to his assistant, 'when they sing like that, what's it mean?' Bert smiled and shrugged his shoulders. 'I don't know what the words mean,' he said, 'but I reckon they're just saying, well, they're just saying they're happy, I reckon.' 'Ha!' said the fore-man, 'that's what they're saying. I wish we could sing the same!'

It is many a long year since the Big Hole was abandoned, and now only the tourists peer into its cavity or are photographed beside Rhodes's railway carriage, which stands in polished floridity near the edge of the pit. Kimberley is still a great diamond producer, though. It is dominated by the mining company of De Beers, a subsidiary of the mammoth Anglo-American

156

Corporation (of which its late chairman, Sir Ernest Oppenheimer, once remarked with noble clarity: 'It was founded to make profits for its shareholders, and the undertakings that the corporation embarks upon are those that hold out prospects of reward'). Kimberley's rewards have been so substantial and so consistent that on any day of the week (so I was assured) there are £1m. worth of jewels in the De Beers offices.

Splendid, old-school, wood-panelled, gentlemanly offices they are; and since this is still largely a company town, they are the real centre of its doings and its loyalties. Pretorians may revolve about their statue of President Kruger. To Kimberley people De Beers is the symbol of their identity. The offices are built rather in the style of those old Suez Canal Company buildings that used to dignify the harum-scarum streets of Suez and Port Said: that is to say, they have a slightly snooty, stiff-upper-lip look to them, as though they were used to better things, and only sticking it out for the good of the shareholders. Their rooms are elderly and brownly muffled, and upon the walls there hang innumerable photographs—magnates in frock-coats and bowlers, groups of directors in diagonal postures, Rhodes himself with his habitual quizzical sneer. You will be taken upstairs to a powerful man in shirt-sleeves; you will ask him diffidently if there's any chance of seeing a diamond mine; you will add hastily that you realize Mondays and Fridays are visiting days, but you are leaving on Wednesday; and in a trice you will find yourself bowling towards the mine in a big black car, with a pass in your pocket and an appointment kindly made by telephone.

The most interesting thing about a diamond mine is its need for perpetual vigilance. Unless you happen to possess a gold reduction plant, it is not much use stealing a bit of reef from a gold mine: but a diamond needs no primary processing, it is small and compact and infinitely alluring, and it is often all too easy to recognize. There are men of dubious enterprise who come especially to Kimberley from the Rand to steal a single stone: they sign on with De Beers, undergo the usual period of training, acquire their diamond (if they can), sell it on the intricate underground market, and go back to bus conducting, the

157

richer by a Cadillac. A labyrinthine international organization, rich in romance, does its best to block the channels of subterfuge by which these stolen diamonds find their way to the markets of the world. You may not suppose, as you race through the out-skirts of Kimberley, that there is any very direct connection be-tween this hot little, raw little city and the scented sophistica-tions of Beirut: but ask a diamond detective, or whisper a dis-creet inquiry to one of the Lebanese millionaires, and you will soon know better. Except perhaps for a seductive perfume, nothing symbolizes temptation more exactly than the prismatic glitter of a diamond, sharp, precise and bitter: and a perpetual temptation the gem remains, so that the gentlest of citizens, as he passes through the barrier at the mine gate, sometimes finds himself plotting an armed assault, or wondering how many carats would hide behind his hatband.

A plateau of bleak no-man's-land surrounds your mine at Kimberley, and within this area are confined the African mine-workers. Highly-trained Alsatians patrol it and armed men guard its exits. Within its fences the whole process of diamond production is conducted. There are the mine-shafts (for it is underground mining nowadays, down the deep diamondiferous pipes); and there are the big crushers which pound the rock when it comes to the surface (so hard are the diamonds that they are hardly ever broken in this brutal process); and there are the little trains which, clanking mildly, bring the crushed rock to the washing plant; and there is the series of pots and pans and weirs and screens that reduce the crushed, washed, sorted rock to the smallest concentrates. Finally they extract the diamonds. In a long unpretentious room, not unlike a printing shop, there stand a series of machines like linotypes. Five or six elderly operators, of unspeakable integrity, tend these machines and greet the visitor with grave incorruptible smiles. The crushed rock arrives down a chute and is poured over a sloping table lined with petroleum jelly: and if you watch this operation very closely, and scrupulously obey the instructions of the machine-man, you may see a petit-point of tiny speckles ornamenting the surface of the grease. The muck runs away out of sight, to be

DIAMONDS

returned to the earth again: but the diamonds, those unshakable cores of brilliance, embed themselves in the vaseline like
oysters, and sparkle away merrily when the operator, seizing a
trowel, scrapes the grease from his table and deposits it in a
nearby pot.

So they get their diamonds. The grease is boiled away and
next door four men and a girl, in clinical white coats, pick up
the gems in frying-pans and sort them on a table. There are
greenish diamonds and yellow ones, brown and white and an
occasional heavenly blue: there are little flaky unpretentious
diamonds, and diamonds that seem to have been chipped with a
penknife, and diamonds of an ultimate perfection of symmetry.
They examine these treasures with their eye-glasses, and they
sort them by shape and colour: but at the end of the day, for all
the sweat of the black miners and the rattling of the trucks, the
swilling and the washing and the shaking and the crushing and
the greasing and the boiling and the sorting, only two little piles
of stones, like magical molehills, lie on that table complacently.

How easy it would be, I thought shiftily, to grab a pile and
run for it! But an overwhelming sense of honesty pervaded that
sorting-room and made me blush in shame: and when I asked
one of the men if he ever had such subversive thoughts, he spoke
in almost canonical tones about his gratitude to the company,
his thirty-eight years of happy service, the generosity and en-
lightenment of De Beers and the unutterable goodness of Sir
Ernest Oppenheimer. When I quoted him to a rude miner downstairs, though, outside this rarefied circle of devotion, that artisan
put me more at my ease: 'Ho yes!' said he. 'I know them. They'd
pinch the whole bloody lot if they thought they could get away
with it!' And getting away with it, indeed, does seem to be difficult, especially for an African. Various inducements are offered
him to prevent him stealing diamonds anyway. If he picks one
up and hands it piously to the management he is handsomely
rewarded, sometimes so well that he can end his contract and go
home to Basutoland in triumph. He is always well fed, well
housed, kindly looked after. The flesh is human, though, and
the company is aware that unswerving devotion to one's em-

159

ployer is not a universal emotion. The African miner is therefore carefully confined within the compound for the duration of his contract. In the old days company inspectors purged him heavily at the end of his contract, to prevent him secreting diamonds in his guts; and they also, for a few days before his departure, imprisoned his hands in huge unwieldy gloves, to prevent him handling small objects of any kind—there were slits in the gloves for knives and forks, but otherwise he was helpless with anything smaller than a pickaxe.

Nowadays the methods are less barbaric but more efficient. The miner is thoroughly X-rayed before he leaves. If there is a suspicious blob in his kidneys they wait for a few days and X-ray him again, to see if it has moved. If he has cut a slit in his arm and hidden a diamond inside his skin, they painlessly remove it. If he has deposited one under his tongue they patiently instruct him to spit it out. Only a few flamboyant rogues defeat the system by sleight-of-hand or brazen cunning, and some people say that most of the thieving nowadays is done by white miners, who are less carefully screened: but a few endearing Africans take a mischievous pleasure in misleading the authorities by swallowing bits of valueless crystal, or boiling glass so thoroughly in condensed milk that it acquires the peculiar greasy sheen of the diamond (like the soft enticing sheen of melting snow that you may sometimes see, a patch of watered silk, high on a mountain flank).

The white worker may be searched, but not X-rayed, and that is how he sometimes buys his Cadillac. Even in the flexible milieu of Kimberley, where it is hard to imagine a race riot or a bus boycott, racial prejudices sometimes intrude. In one mine building, as I chatted with a friendly foreman and returned the grins of the passing Africans, I happened to observe an old notice upon the wall, written in ornate Edwardian script, not unlike the writing on that monumental cheque. 'Before Starting The Winch', it said, with an obscurely evangelical air, 'Operators Must Ensure That Neither Men Nor Natives are In the Vicinity.'

20

ON MISCEGENATION

Let us think for a moment about miscegenation. Nearly everyone else in South Africa does. Some people talk about it. A desperate few even miscegenate (if that is the verb). One of the ultimate causes of apartheid and baaskap and the other racial phenomena of the Union is the fear of cross-breeding, either individual ('poor Cousin Ethel, you know what became of her') or national ('If we weaken, we shall become a coffee-coloured society'). Just as in the southern states of America, almost every argument on racial theory leads us in the end, however resolutely we try to by-pass the issue, to that inevitable old faithful: 'How would you feel if your sister'—or daughter, or brother, or son, according to your age, sex and circumstance—'how would you feel if your nearest and dearest married a Kaffir?' If you are an average honest western visitor, you will probably say, well, you wouldn't actually mind, if that's what she really wanted, it's her happiness that counts, etc. etc. If you are brash and argumentative, and perhaps wear a duffle-coat or pink lipstick, you will say there's nothing in the world that would please you better, some of these black people seem such splendid upstanding men. If you are cautious and analytical, you will say er, um, yes, of course it isn't the biological aspect, so to speak, that might cause you a little anxiety, but what one might describe as the *sociological* aspect, ours being a society, alas, not yet adapted to the interfloriation of young persons of, er, different, er, pigments.

But the truth is that a great many of us, whatever our political or social opinions, dislike the idea of black flesh cleaving to white (as is, I believe, the technical, or at least the Biblical description of the process). A great many more have an instinc-

ON MISCEGENATION

tive distaste for half-castes, however worthy, and a contempt for
those mongrel people whose inter-breeding is unluckily apparent
in the colour of their skins. The confused origins of the English
are a matter of pride; but let us be honest, most of us are not
wildly attracted by the Egyptians. There is an intelligent school
of thought in South Africa, led by daredevil liberals, which maintains that general miscegenation is the answer to the Union's
problems; that only uninhibited sexual intercourse between the
races can properly cement economic and social union. To the
old-school South African, Afrikaner or British, this argument is
absolute anathema, and he blocks his ears to it as a cardinal
might reject the blandishments of Luther. To the educated
African, on the other hand, it often sounds mildly deranged,
because (tastes being what they are) it seems unlikely ever
to be fulfilled—most white girls prefer white men, most black
men black girls. And to the rest of us, safely immune to the
anxieties of Africa? I opened my window this very morning
and put the question to half a dozen passing villagers, and found
that we in England are still much nearer the predikant than the
ligers of Bloemfontein.

Miscegenation is most pertinently considered in Cape Province, for here there lives a large and thriving society of half-
castes, traditionally (and confusingly) called Cape Coloureds.
Those sozzled wine-farm labourers were Coloureds, and so are
many of the artisans of the Cape, the bus-drivers and policemen,
the garage-hands, the postmen. They are, by and large, an intelligent people. Some have risen to positions of distinction and
responsibility. Others are among the most embittered politicians
of the Union, and produce a weekly newspaper of rock-bottom
pseudo-Marxist drabness. The Coloured people have always
felt themselves much closer to the whites than to the blacks, and
indeed were for generations treated as such; but the Nationalist
Government determined to deprive them of their traditional
rights to vote on a common roll with the Europeans. So resolved
were the Nationalists to force through this cruel act of racial
discrimination that they especially enlarged the Senate in order
to circumvent the constitutional difficulties. If they have any

162

doubts about its effect upon the Coloureds, they have only to thumb through the pages of that weekly newspaper and observe the spleen and sense of wrong that animates its every paragraph.

The Cape Coloureds are an extraordinary mixture of stocks. Some of their ancestors were Malay slaves, imported by the Dutch in the seventeenth century. Some were the free-living seamen who came to the Cape from every nation in its early days of settlement. Some were undoubtedly Dutch or British officials. And some were what our benevolent great-aunts used to call, in writing out the collection figures for the church porch, 'Hottentots'. There is very little black blood in the Coloureds, because when the first Europeans came to the Cape there were no black men there. The only inhabitants were a shy little race of Bushmen, dubbed the Hottentots (so they say) after the Dutch word for 'stammerer', the most pathetic etymological derivation I know. Figuratively, as the *Oxford Dictionary* says with a sniff, a Hottentot is 'a person of inferior intellect or culture'. ('Is it possible to love such a man?' asked Chesterfield of Lord Lyttelton. 'No. The utmost I can do for him is to consider him a respectable Hottentot.') Poor little Bushmen. They seem to have been, for all their blowpipes and poisons, a relatively harmless folk, more diffident than murderous. With their stutters and their scamperings and their governors' mistresses, they reach to us through the generations with an endearing quaintness (though the Cape Coloured, it need hardly be said, is much prouder of his sailors' blood than he is of his Hottentot).

A few Bushmen survive to this day in the desolate expanses of South-West Africa. An Afrikaner policeman once told me of his difficulties in handling them. They were a slippery, crab-like little people, he said, extraordinarily difficult to master. Their limbs were so small that they could easily slip out of the standard handcuffs, so they had to put the cuffs on their ankles instead. The Bushmen have two kinds of weapon: a full-sized bow and arrow which is their equivalent of the rifle; and a sort of hand bow, small but lethal, which might be compared to those glistening bejewelled automatics that are so often to be found, if we believe the thrillers, tucked among hankies in satin handbags.

ON MISCEGENATION

'You never saw such people,' said the policeman. 'I charged one once with murdering another fellow. He was very annoyed, said he'd killed two of them, he wasn't going to be accused of murdering just one, dear me no!'

You can see for yourself what the Hottentots were like in a remarkable exhibit at the Cape Town Museum. Before the last Hottentots disappeared from the Cape, casts were taken of their entire bodies: and there they stand in immortality, immured behind plate-glass in the museum ('Foodstuffs, Peanuts, etc.,' says a notice outside, 'Not Allowed to Be Eaten in This Museum'). They are all extremely small, and almost white, and appear intelligent but baffled. The women have buttocks of grotesque enormity, giving them an almost bestial appearance, though they apparently did not repel those lascivious sailors of old; and the men have strange little squashed features, lined and frowning and obscurely sophisticated, making them look like minute ill-orientated Somerset Maughams. I never saw a queerer people, even behind plate-glass, and I shall never read that Coloured newspaper again without recalling the contributors' putative ancestors, peering back at me so solemnly from the recesses of the museum.

Nowadays, of course, the possibility of intercourse with a Hottentot woman is remote, and your male fancies must be esoteric indeed to entice you all the way to Abenab or Otji-warongo for the pleasure. The Cape Coloureds themselves often do their best to pass as whites, and a million are said to have achieved permanent apotheosis. They would certainly hesitate before forming alliances with Africans. Europeans are sometimes less fastidious, if that is not an offensive word. Several old down-and-outs, thickened with gin and squalor, enjoy their satisfactions in the locations of Durban and the Rand. In Johannesburg there is at least one brothel dedicated to the illicit joys of miscegenation, and in Sophiatown there is a celebrated white woman who has renounced her colour altogether, insists that she is black in culture and instinct, and lives with a black protector in the very heart of the African area. When she once appeared in court, the judge remarked portentously that

ON MISCEGENATION

'Regina Brooke was not a European within the meaning of the Act'.

For miscegenation is illegal in South Africa. It has been illegal outside matrimony since 1927, and since 1949 mixed marriages have been prohibited, too. The maximum penalty for an offence is six months' hard labour, and that is what offenders nearly always get. On the subject of inter-racial intercourse public opinion, black and white, is always lively and always intense. 'Wow!' wrote a columnist in *Drum*, during my winter in South Africa. 'I've just got the true facts behind the tragic suicide of luscious Queen Mehlomakulu of George Goch, Johannesburg. You remember the red-hot pin-up who shocked us by bathing herself in paraffin and setting herself on fire? Everybody wanted to know what the blazes she did it for. So I give. Queen was going to have a baby . . . by a white. She panicked and burned herself to death. That's the story behind her tragic words, "It's too late . . . it's done!" ' Many another tragedy, immune to the glare of razzle-dazzle journalism, ruins the lives of African families or haunts the memories of Europeans. A sexual attraction often exists between blacks and whites in the Union, though the Bantu tribes-people are not (to an impartial European eye) nearly as attractive as the handsome peoples of Ghana and Nigeria, where miscegenation has a long and tolerated record. White people in the Union often believe blacks to possess extra virility: black people think the same about whites. There is an adventure and a stimulation to this forbidden intercourse, and an exciting sense of disparity between the partners. If you ever run to earth one of those white ne'er-do-wells of the location shebeens, he will tell you between his draughts of liquor that there is no woman like a Kaffir woman, no sir, nowhere in the world. And indeed, most tragic of all, liaisons of genuine love do arise between Europeans and Africans in the Union, pre-destined to calamity, as fated and ill-starred as any Pinkerton's romance or the passions of an Othello.

Sometimes such pitiful affairs bind together a white man and a girl who, though Coloured, can pass as white. This is perhaps the most terrible of the racial predicaments of South Africa, for the girl is constantly haunted by the possibility of discovery. Desperate are the measures she may take to bolster her security. She treats her hair with lotions to remove its kinks. She plasters her face with make-up, to hide that subtle ingrained trace of darkness. Perhaps she answers the advertisement of some unscrupulous chemist, and spends her money on creams to change the pigmentation of her skin. She listens to her own voice in the privacy of her bedroom, to pounce upon any trace of the African's cheerful singsong. She dresses with unnatural restraint to avoid the stigma of the African's flamboyance. When she sits with her lover in a European restaurant, she fancies that the eyes of the room are upon her, searching her skin and her hair and her bearing for the tell-tale signs that could send her in misery and ignominy before the courts: and when the policeman walks by, and looks her coolly up and down, from her curls to her high heels, she shares the momentary sickening self-doubt of all criminals or transgressors, when the cold eye of the law is upon them. Worst of all, she dreads this: that when at last they produce a child, born out of all these travails and anxieties, it will be not white, or even mulatto, but brazenly, uncompromisingly, gloriously black, and thus betray her not only to the police and the mother-in-law, but even to the husband.

In the early days of the South African experiment no such prudish legalities separated the sperms and ovaries of the races. Even the pious Dutch colonists, in the early days of settlement, took Hottentot wives and reared half-caste babies. An insidious touch of the tar-brush smears the racial purity of many a self-righteous Afrikaner, and there are political propagandists who have proved to their own extreme satisfaction that almost every member of the Government has black blood in his veins. Certainly one encounters some vociferous Nationalists, and respectable Opposition spokesmen, too, who are patently dark of skin and crinkly of hair. (I once went to present a letter of introduction to a woman who worked in an art gallery. Another woman, one of her colleagues, greeted me at the reception desk and examined me, I thought, with inadequately concealed suspicion. I explained my business. 'Mary,' she called through the door, 'there's a young man here to see you': and she added in a dark, monitory and ill-suppressed undertone: 'My dear, he's got *very* curly hair!')

So there is scarcely a facet of human intercourse in South Africa, from the blatantly public to the intimately hushed, that does not suffer from the decrees and judgment of racial theory. Apartheid affects every activity, distorts every opinion, dominates conversations, fills the newspapers, jams the cables, separates the suburbs, bisects the buses, and keeps the mills of controversy endlessly tediously turning. It even lays its chill finger upon the universal fundamentals, and stares, like a guardian eunuch through a grille, upon the privacies of the body. 'Is making love work or pleasure?' asks the stooge in an old South African joke. 'Pleasure,' says the black comedian. 'If it was work the baas would make me do it.'

21

PARLIAMENT

The Civil Service lords it in Pretoria, among the jacaranda trees; the judiciary cogitates among its stinkwood in Bloemfontein; but the Parliament of the Union of South Africa meets, as it should, in the mother city of Cape Town. The Assembly sits in a grand but rather deadening palace, surrounded by gardens in the shadow of Table Mountain, and of all the Parliaments I have ever encountered, it is the most sensibly and informally run. Here is none of the gold-laced aloofness of Westminster, nor any of the hastily assumed tradition that gives an unavoidable air of silliness to the new assemblies of Rhodesia, the Sudan, Ghana and Nigeria. South Africa has been independent for half a century, and has long been a power in her own right, so that this is no pallid imitation of the House of Commons. It is the easiest thing in the world to get a ticket for the public gallery; and it is even easier to see your M.P., for you merely walk through the door, tap a lackey on the shoulder, give him your card and smile nicely: and in a trice you are in the restaurant, drinking parliamentary tea and eating the party line. Perhaps because there are four provincial assemblies as well, the M.P. is not quite so big a wig as he is in England, and he is certainly much less pretentious. (Again we hear the echo of the frontier: and as you walk into the lobby of the House you may irreverently imagine yourself, if you enjoy that kind of fancy, bursting through the swing-doors of a smoky gold-rush saloon, summoning a whisky or a madam.)

Alas, the proceedings of the assembly are not so breezily encouraging: and indeed, with its pompous declamations and its childish witticisms, its bickerings and its showings off, a session

PARLIAMENT

of the Union Parliament can be a depressing experience. This is partly because of the gloomy patina of racial anxiety; and partly because of the overwhelming power of the Government, so predominant that the Nationalist benches spill heavily into the Opposition side of the House; but chiefly, perhaps, because of the generally low calibre of the members. For a population of its size, white South Africa has a quite remarkable number of gifted and impressive men: but not many of them stand for Parliament.

Nevertheless, there is often an element of drama, and sometimes of pathos, to this ill-starred House. In the public gallery, day in and day out, there sit two women representing the Black Sash organization. They listen in attitudes of mournful protest, and since they are forbidden to flaunt their sashes in the House, they wear long black gloves instead, and sometimes hold them diagonally across their breasts, thus effectively circumventing the Speaker's ruling. There are often solemn rows of children up there, too, and perhaps a few provincial visitors clutching guide-books; and in a small niche beside this gallery one or two Africans may sometimes be seen in subdued and respectful segregation. In the press gallery, at the other end of the House, the corps of reporters seems to be dominated by young men with beards: a beard has become a symbol of Afrikaner manhood, and if there is a bearded journalist there with an English name and an Opposition tone of voice, it is because, as he will tell you, he wants to prove 'the Nats haven't got a patent on the damn things'. A few foreign correspondents sit cynically at their benches, if it is an important debate, and sometimes saunter out with books under their arms for a reviving cup of coffee in St. George's Street, or an exchange of despondencies.

For the floor of the House is generally uncompelling. Members talk partly in English, partly in Afrikaans: that is to say, the Nationalists nearly always speak in Afrikaans, and the United Party members nearly always speak in English—though when there is some occasion for a sickly patriotic demonstration, the granting of a pension to some innocuous worthy, a tribute to some universally respected (because thoroughly dead)

169

national celebrity, the parties sometimes unctuously reverse their instincts and speak each other's languages. The aesthetics of the chamber are marred by an infestation of hanging microphones and by an incongruous glass roof like a railway station's (when a cloud passes overhead an electric eye switches on the lights); but its general physical atmosphere is conventional enough, leather-backed and sombrely panelled, and at first glance this might be any provincial civic council meeting to discuss the rates. Few pungent eccentrics lounge along these benches or attract the cartoonists. Only occasionally does some rotund reverberating phrase give style to the discussions. It is often difficult to believe that currents of bitter venom, tragedy and idealism animate the affairs of this assembly, or that some of the ministers down there, prosaic enough in their double-breasted suits, are among the most universally detested men on earth.

Of the two major parties below you, as you lean over the gallery above the clock, it is undoubtedly the Nationalists that will more persistently engage your interest. They will not much attract you, or even impress you perhaps, but there is something about their demeanour that is obscurely fascinating. An air of discipline hovers over their benches. It is as though an irresistible bond has united them in some mystical brotherhood, making them look, for all their variances of age and physique (not of sex, for they are all men) inexplicably alike. There is an earnest rigidity to their bearing, and a glitter to their eyes. Critics sometimes say that the Nationalist Party is not a political party at all in the English sense of the term, but rather a shield or camouflage for something far less flexible—for the Broederbond, for Afrikaner nationalism, for the spirit of the Volk itself; and indeed sometimes as you watch those parliamentarians at work the thought may cross your mind that they are all puppets of some off-stage manipulator, or digits in an adding machine.

In the front benches sit the ministers, busily engaged in demarcating the frontiers of apartheid: Strijdom, the Prime Minister, a stocky, strong-looking man with a dull but determined face; 'Blackie' Swart, a genial giant, who once brandished a cat-o'-nine-tails on this very floor; Theophilus Donges, reputed

170

to be a man of more sophisticated power; Eric Louw, a rather whining Minister of External Affairs; and deep in a pile of papers and notes, the notorious Dr. Verwoerd, Minister of Native Affairs, whose god-like zeal is devoted entirely to dividing black from white from coloured from Indian. These men form a resolute, united but fearfully boring team, and the party behind them is united too, and very confident. A perennial phenomenon of South African politics is the tendency of the Afrikaners to form splinter groups, and indeed while I was in South Africa one such party was created by a rebel Nationalist: but there is no welding force so potent as power. So long as apartheid was good politics, it seemed to me during my winter in the Union, the Nationalist Party would remain a well-marshalled entity.

It is revealing to talk to some of these Government backbenchers, from Bloemfontein or Rustenberg, the High Veldt or the Karoo. A Cape Afrikaner may be surprisingly adaptable in his opinions: but there is nobody more dogmatic than an upcountry Boer politician, with all his republican background and Calvinist breeding. Time and again, as you gossip in the lobbies, you will hear the catch-phrases of discrimination, delivered with an air at once firm and understanding, like a headmaster pleading with a promising but recalcitrant pupil. 'It's a matter of sheer survival . . . morality of self-defence . . . best for the natives in the long run . . . of course you can't understand, you haven't lived here . . . choice of apartheid or integration . . . we're not bullies, you know, we believe in the Word of God . . . disgraceful foreign misrepresentation . . . shocking misreporting . . . miscegenation . . . we'll be swamped . . . mixed society . . . coffee-coloured . . . swamped . . . fungus, you know . . . ox-wagons . . . totally swamped . . . and how would you feel, anyway, if your sister married one? Eh, tell me honestly, how would you feel then?' All the old familiars are summoned, the same old arguments, the tired appeals to realism and to history. Two other shades of thought, though, may surprise you by their intrusion. One is a suggestion of bland and unrepentant hypocrisy, a subtle hinted admission that all they really want is plain baaskap—the metaphysical shadow of a wink, as much as to say, 'Of course, man, we know this is all eyewash, and we know that you know that we know!' The other is even more disconcerting. It is a streak of petulance, such as gypsies and Irishmen sometimes employ when, all their bluff and blarney having failed, they suddenly fall back upon a patter of sentimental self-pity. Suddenly your parliamentarian's face, dropping its masks of dogma or complicity, will assume an expression of maudlin appeal. He will tug at his little black Afrikaner beard, and look you in the eyes soulfully, and then he will say in a slightly throaty voice: 'But, man, don't you see, all we ask is a little sympathy? All we need is fairness and fair play from the world. All we seek is the tolerance and sympathy of friends. Is that too much to ask?'

Different indeed is the atmosphere of the United Party, which sprawls impotently on the opposite side of the House. This is a much less homogeneous affair. Some of its members are Afrikaner renegades of distinction. Some are charming Cape dilettantes. A plethora of stage Englishmen makes its speeches in affected accents, wearing school ties and button-holes. Theirs is the milieu of the road-house or the fumed-oak bar, where beery men with bogus vowels talk incessantly about their war experiences, and flirt unsuccessfully with the barmaid. The few women on the Opposition benches look cool and elegant: but the men often smack heavily of the morning after the night before. It is entertaining to visit the Assembly late in the evening, after the dinner adjournment. The Nationalists still sit there in tight-lipped phalanx, spouting their Afrikaans forcefully into the microphones; but a languid feeling of *laissez-faire* has overcome the Opposition, and its members laze about in an aura of brandy and cigars, and make frequent ribald interruptions, and laugh a great deal at their own jokes and the futile interjections of their friends. Sometimes they like to make a show of their democratic instincts, especially if there are distinguished visitors in the gallery, and I remember with distaste a little episode that occurred one day when Mr. Adlai Stevenson was visiting the Assembly. A United Party member, dressed more or less in the fashion of a pre-war juvenile lead, evidently wished to demonstrate his breadth of vision: so in the middle of a debate, and with a careful glance at the gallery, he rose from his seat and adjusted his tie; and stepped stiffly into the aisle, his thumbs on the seams of his trousers; and bowed with exaggerated dignity to the Speaker; and then, with a gesture of supreme political tolerance, hitched his trousers up and sat down in the Government front bench beside a Nationalist acquaintance—who, evidently wondering what in the world was happening, put on his glasses and stared at his colleague with unconcealed astonishment. I do not know if Mr. Stevenson observed this little by-play: but it was worth seeing, if only as an example of a dying school of John Barrymore acting.

The feebler United Party members rely heavily for their effects upon fruity humour, sarcasm, and a kind of ineffectual disdain. They share innumerable private jokes among themselves, sometimes adapting them for articles in the newspapers later, and they are apt to sit down suddenly, after discharging one of these sallies, ignoring the laughter and looking fixedly at the ceiling in the familiar manner of bar-room raconteurs. They are fond of throwing a point into the debate and then pausing for a moment, eyebrows raised, face blank, head nodding slightly, while the Government is supposedly reeling from its effect; and they like to refer, if they can, to the 'inexperience' of the previous speaker. 'We shall make allowances', they will say, looking at each other with ironic smiles, 'for the youth and inexperience of the Honourable Member, and we must bear in mind that at the time we are discussing, when my Honourable Friend here had the privilege, if I remember rightly, of acting as G.S.O. 3 to the 2nd Infantry Division, at that stirring time the Honourable Member on the opposite side of the House was, if indeed out of the nursery, still no more than a schoolboy. And the Honourable Member will perhaps forgive me, Mr. Speaker, if I add that in the opinion of myself and many of my colleagues on this side of the House, the Honourable Member is still little more than an inexperienced schoolboy now!' (And during one of these cadences, if the speaker is exceptionally fervent, or more bitterly stung by his opponent than he cares to admit, it is interesting to observe how his posh public school accent degenerates, over the subordinate clauses, to something distinctly related to the dialects of those dear old souls in the coffee-bar in Johannesburg!)

There are exceptions to all these dismal rules. Sir De Villiers Graaf, the leader of the Opposition, is a man of singular charm and graceful bearing. Some of the Afrikaner back-benchers, on the Opposition side, are able and witty. One of the United Party women was described to me by a connoisseur as the most attractive woman in South Africa. And sometimes (during my Union winter) a queer and magnetic figure would enter the House through its curtained entrance, sidle past the young serjeant-at-arms, and bow awkwardly to the Speaker. His was a diffident, lopsided appearance, and he walked in a slightly crab-like movement, as if overcome by shyness or respect. His suit was nondescript, his tie crookedly tucked under his collar, and his shoes looked as though they might very well need re-heeling: and yet, as you watched him walk to his seat among the mediocrities, there was to his presence an unmistakable sense of bigness and significance. He brought to the Assembly a suggestion of power and authority, and leavened its pitifully provincial manners as a Churchill or Bevan gives stature to the House of Commons. This was no chance impression. In 1957 Harry Oppenheimer was not only the clearest thinker in the United Party, the ultimate source of much of its finance, and a champion of common-sense moderation: he was at the same time the greatest of the gold magnates, the chairman of a dozen companies, and one of the richest and most powerful private citizens on earth. Now he has succeeded his father at the head of the Anglo-American Corporation and has abandoned politics: but when I was in Cape Town he made everyone else in the Assembly dull by comparison.

But dull is perhaps the wrong word. Sometimes this Assembly, especially in its moments of defiance, seems inspired with a sombre lunacy, as though it represents the electors of some grand and gloomy never-never land. Let me recall to you, as an example, a foreign policy speech delivered by Mr. Louw to a packed House. Now it is normal for Foreign Ministers to include in their public statements an occasional friendly reference to allied Powers or sympathetic states, some soothing expression of diplomacy, perhaps, a tribute to the United Nations or a word of condescension to the Commonwealth. This is the prudent, conciliatory way, sliding often into platitudes and hypocrisies, but honouring a useful and well-tried formula. It is not, however, the contemporary South African practice. To the Nationalist Government, everything is either black or white. You are either with South Africa or against her. You are either a saint or a blackguard. This is unfortunate for Mr. Louw, because as it happens not a single Power in the world, not an international agency, not a faith or a fraternity supports South Africa in her complex delusions of rectitude.

So within a few moments the Minister for External Affairs had effectively insulted half the world. He mocked the United Nations. He defied the Bandung bloc. He was hostile to the Soviet Union. He was patronizing about Ghana. He accused an American Congressional mission of 'uncalled for and improper intrusion'. Not a breath of compromise entered his speech, not a shadow of an admission that the whole world, black, brown and white, Communist and capitalist, pagan and devout, was united in its conviction that the Union's racial policies were mistaken. Everyone was out of step but our Johnnie, proclaimed the minister, but we're the king of the castle, we're the king of the castle. His Nationalist colleagues listened respectfully during his performance: and his United Party opponents, though they interrupted him now and then, looked as though they were counting the minutes till opening time.

22

AUTOCRACY

Is South Africa a police state? It may not seem very probable, as you march so jauntily in and out of Parliament, or accost a passing minister, or chuckle at the latest scurrilous cartoon of Dr. Verwoerd. During my South African winter, all the same, it could be seriously suggested that we were witnessing the twilight of democracy in the Dominion, that the old traditions of frontier freedom were being systematically destroyed, and that there would never again be genuinely free parliamentary elections. Everyone could see how cross-grained the Government was, how ham-handed and obstinate; and there were many to remember that some of its ministers used to be enthusiastic supporters of the Nazi cause. 'They just don't believe in individual freedom,' I was told time and again, 'they're only interested in the supremacy of the Volk.'

Of course for the Africans of the country this is undeniably a police state, in an extreme sense of an ominous phrase. The black men of South Africa, whatever their individual attainments and character, have virtually no rights at all: this is taxation without responsibility carried to an almost ludicrous excess. Every African in the Union lives under the shadow of arbitrary arrest and prosecution. The pass system and the multifarious laws of apartheid restrict his movements, even denying him, in some circumstances, the right to live with his wife; the labour laws prevent him, however intelligent or educated he is, from improving his position; there are thousands of public buildings to which he is forbidden access; and he will be an exceedingly lucky Kaffir if he ever gets a passport. For four-fifths of the Union's population this is authoritarianism with a vengeance.

AUTOCRACY

For the white minority it remains a curiously schizophrenic state. In some respects it bears all the hall-marks of autocracy; in others it is liberal enough. For example, during my stay in the Union there was no trace of a censorship. Foreign correspondents might be reproached or corrected, but they could cable exactly what they pleased. The Opposition press was vividly outspoken. It is true that a commission had been examining the press (concluding *inter alia*, that the *Manchester Guardian's* reports on South African affairs were 'accurate, but of a liberal bias') and that many people expected new legislation to govern the newspapers. But I take with a pinch of salt the more horrifying stories of press intimidation. Public discussion in the Union is still free. Ministers are easy to see and disagree with. The Government talks with foolish petulance of foreign misrepresentation, but does not try to stifle it (there is perhaps an element of masochism to the enmeshed neuroses of the Afrikaner).

On the other hand, I doubt whether the average Afrikaner is, *au fond*, a genuinely democratic animal. The British South African often turns a blind eye to the miseries of the African, but at least he feels strongly and sincerely about the liberty of Europeans. The Afrikaner, I sometimes think does not suffer from this particular dichotomy because he does not really grasp the nuances of democratic principle. He will often tell you how democratic were the old Boer republics, and recall with pride the free-and-easy, almost anarchical methods of the hard-riding commandos: but if ever you hear him discussing the failings of the jury system, or the degradations of public disagreement, or the shameful weakness of a democracy divided upon principle, you will realize that his conceptions of private and public freedom are alien to yours, and much less generous.

Nobody yet knows whether the Nationalist leaders will ever translate these innate prejudices into a new structure of government. The Afrikaner politicians are not always as heavily consistent as they seem, and their aims and techniques sometimes fluctuate disconcertingly. At one end of their scale of behaviour, as people are quick to point out, there is a coarseness and arro-

177

gance which could certainly develop into totalitarianism. The Black Sash branch in Cape Town once wrote to Dr. Donges, Minister of the Interior, to ask for reassurances that recent African protests against legislation would not lead to reprisals, as the Africans themselves feared. The Black Sash, said the letter politely, felt sure that no reprisals would occur, but on behalf of the Africans concerned would welcome official assurances, just the same. This was the ministry's reply, on official writing paper: 'I am directed by Dr. the Hon. T. E. Donges to acknowledge receipt of your letter in regard to the petition relative to the proclamation of Group Areas Act in the Cape Peninsula and to state that the questions posed by you on behalf of certain unmentioned people reveal a mentality so puerile and senile or just plainly malicious that they do not deserve a reply. From your remark that "you are satisfied that the fears of these people are not justified" it would appear that you are agreed as to the fatuity of these questions.' Imagine such a reply from the Home Secretary in England, directed with an official frank to the Society for the Abolition of Wickedness (which indeed, so imprecise are the purposes of the Black Sash, that well-meaning organization sometimes seems to resemble).

Then there are the various measures which, though designed basically to bolster apartheid, could affect white people as seriously as they do blacks. The most far-reaching of these is the Suppression of Communism Act, which defines Communism so loosely that almost any opponent of racial segregation can be charged under it—and further charged, if the Johannesburg Treason Trial is anything to go by, with treason. You have only to be 'named' as a Communist by a government-appointed official to be assumed guilty of the accusation: you are then disqualified from Parliament and may be prohibited from attending public gatherings. You can be banished from any particular area. If you were not born in South Africa you can be deported. If you were, you can be deprived of your passport, and thus forbidden either to leave the country for good or to make a specific journey abroad (while I was in the Union a former mayor of Johannesburg was prevented from attending a Commonwealth

Labour Conference in London, and a distinguished novelist was forbidden to visit his publishers in England).

Telephone tapping is commonplace in South Africa. (Many a Nationalist asked me gleefully about the fuss over a case of tapping in England, not realizing that the very intensity of the fuss was a measure of the rarity of the tapping: in the same way they often stupidly quote in their own defence the opinions of those cross-patched and ill-bred English landladies who are sometimes pictured in the Sunday papers turning black students away from their unenticing premises.) Sometimes people complain that their mail has been opened. A woman writer told me that the manuscript of one of her books had been stolen by police agents masquerading as meter readers. In Pretoria, they were complaining that a list of Broederbond members had been mysteriously removed from a liberal's house. The Europeans accused in the treason trial were arrested in the middle of the night and flown off to Johannesburg in military aircraft.

Of course the system of apartheid itself, quite apart from its generally debasing and coarsening effect, imposes potential restrictions on the liberties of Europeans as well as of Africans. The church clause of the Native Laws Amendments Bill, if it is ever enforced, will prevent Europeans from worshipping side by side with Africans. The Universities Apartheid Bill will prevent them from studying with Africans. It may soon be illegal to entertain a black man in your house, as it is already to keep a resident black servant in a proscribed white area. You need a permit to enter some of the black locations, even if you only want to visit a friend there, and you are a criminal if you take him a bottle of brandy. It is not illegal to give an African a lift in your car; but as many kindly Europeans discovered during the Johannesburg bus boycott, there are innumerable ways in which a policeman, inspecting the headlights, counting the number of passengers, measuring the chassis, examining your licence, checking your tax certificate, searching for stolen goods, demanding passes, can irritate, impede or even halt your progress. White opponents of apartheid, few as they are, feel that their country has already deserted the comity of the democracies.

AUTOCRACY

'These stiffs' are not yet totally unscrupulous—far from it: but they seem to be learning fast.

Africaner nationalism, too, is a powerful spur towards autocracy. We have already seen how shamelessly the Nationalist Government packed the Senate to achieve its ends of apartheid: but no less sad, in a country of such noble possibilities, is the parallel packing of the judiciary with good Nationalist Party supporters. Eminent bilingual barristers have been passed over: zealous Nationalist juniors are hastily appointed Queen's Counsel and elevated to the Bench within a few weeks (though, to be fair, the cases I heard tried in South Africa, including the treason trial and many a petty hearing, were conducted with apparent impartiality). There are innumerable instances of unfair political promotions in the Civil Service, from which indeed the British South African is rapidly making a reluctant disappearance. New educational laws restrict the right of the parent to decide the language medium of his child's education. It is improbable that a man with a name like Harrington-Smythe will ever again serve with distinction in the South African Navy, however impeccable his qualifications, visionary his strategy, or original his campaigns against the mole.

There are constant insidious signs that the Government, at the back of its mind, would like to abolish the democratic system in South Africa, establish a republic, and reserve political power to the burghers of Volk. Dr. Donges once remarked in Parliament that already, under existing laws, an elector might be deprived of his vote on economic grounds, or on grounds of religion, and he added that anyway every voter in the Union could be disenfranchised by an ordinary majority of Parliament. This is characteristic of Nationalists' approach to government. They do not necessarily want to impose these autocracies now, but they want to have the power to do so: they are building up a stockpile of legislation, a reserve of domination. If they wish they can manipulate the parliamentary constituencies to ensure a continued Nationalist majority. There is a device called 'delimitation', a local weighting of the vote, which was designed originally to protect country interests against the growing urban preponderance: before every election delimitation commissions decide the boundaries of the constituencies, and since these commissions are officially appointed, it is possible that the Nationalists could thus keep themselves in power indefinitely. 'Dictatorship' is a word often, if rashly, bandied in South Africa.

No wonder the poor old-fashioned Natalians cling to their twin symbols, Crown and Flag, despite the odium of the Nationalists and the sniggers of visiting English liberals. The prospect of an Afrikaner republic is unattractive and the idea of a revived Boer State, with one official language and one accepted master-people, is appalling. Most Afrikaners, I feel sure, do not want such a state: they are willing to live and let live, to tolerate English as a parallel official language, and to retain the existing constitutional arrangements. There is a potent minority, though, which has these neo-Fascist inclinations. It is often forgotten how active was the local Nazi movement during the last war: sabotage was common, if not very effective, and the Ossawa Brandweg was powerful and influential, commanding the loyalties of many prominent Afrikaner citizens. It was only by the narrowest of margins that the South African Parliament voted to enter the war at all, and there were a great many Afrikaners not only convinced that Germany was going to win, but determined to make the most of the fact. To this day Afrikaners will often say that the war against Germany was a terrible mistake: and occasionally, in moments of extreme passion, some old Boer will tell you that he wishes the Germans had won, so there! (And if you disbelieve the latent Afrikaner affinity for Fascism, observe the bearing of one of the traffic policemen who, in their Nazi-like white crash helmets, sometimes strut and swagger among the cars, or sweep by on their motor-cycles with all the cockscomb glamour of the Blackshirts.)

Occasionally, nevertheless, I have doubts about these awful intentions, and about the present Government's propensities for dictatorship. If ever I express them to an Opposition spokesman, he smiles cynically, flicks away his cigarette ash and says with an air of pitying finality: 'My dear chap, if you don't believe me, just take a look at the Nationalist Constitution!' And indeed, this is a disturbing document. It was drawn up by the Nationalists, during the war, in an ill-advised moment of bravado, and it obviously presupposed a Nazi success. As one of the fruits of victory it envisaged a disagreeably authoritarian Afrikaner republic. The existence would be forbidden, it said, of any political organization in strife with the fulfilling of the people's Christian-National vocation. 'White subjects who are acknowledged as members of the state by the Government will be called "burghers" without distinction of race. Such recognition will only be accorded to subjects of whom it can be expected that they will act as builders-up of the nation, whatever status they may have possessed before.' Only burghers would have the right to vote, and a Community Council would be established to deal with the important problems of the country, including, as the document blandly says, 'the poor-white question, the interests of the coloured people, the government of the natives, the Indian penetration, and the surplus Jewish population with excessive economic power'. It makes unpleasant reading: and if, as they claim, the Nationalists have long ago abandoned it as a statement of their ambitions, then they must be either very fickle, or very hypocritical, or possibly both.

Such are some of the symptoms of incipient autocracy in South Africa—from official rudeness at one extreme to this gross constitution at the other, by way of treason trials, telephone tappings, the machinery of apartheid, and a pile of largely unenforced legislation. You may find it hard to credit that all the freedoms are going to be crushed in South Africa, among whites as well as blacks, but this you must accept: that already the Afrikaner leaders think in terms not of individuals, but of groups. 'Go here!' it says to its subject peoples. 'Go there! Blacks on the right, whites on the left! Remove the population from Sophiatown! Charge all those agitators with treason! Strike the Coloureds from the common roll! Insulate the white suburbs! Get those damn Kaffirs out of this end of the railway station!'

AUTOCRACY

Perhaps they are right in so justifying the means by the end. But it would be reassuring to hear the Government saying, one fine South African morning, 'Your obedient servant, Mr. Jones.'

23

MOTHER CITY

It remains a country of paradoxes, and one of the most striking of them is the genial serenity of Cape Town. South Africa is a State charged with menace, suspicion and the rumbles of autocracy, where one of the most awesome of contemporary problems is proceeding in lurches towards some kind of dénouement. But it is also a country of great personal kindness and charm, in which (one sometimes feels) it is only a relatively minor miracle that we need pray for, such as the Venetian painters used to record at the drop of a ducat. Certainly its political capital, reclining in age and grace at the Cape of Good Hope, is one of the pleasure-havens of the earth. If you enter the Union by way of Johannesburg, that brassy cauldron of dilemmas, it is only fair to leave it by way of the Cape; for in Cape Town, if you muffle your consciousness a little, and allow your imagination to overlap your realism, you can conceive what South Africa might be like, were it not for its burdens of tragedy.

In a world of precipitous change the traveller is constantly discovering strange, if hackneyed, transitions: from the oil well to the camel caravan, the cinema to the funeral pyre, rubies to blue jeans. If you like this sort of sensation I recommend to you the contrast between the Union Parliament in Cape Town and the old public gardens that surround it. You will leave the Assembly to the hubbub of the parliamentarians behind you, proposing some new maniacal measure of segregation, flouting the United Nations or squabbling over the Boer War. But the moment you are outside its doors, an idyllic serenity surrounds you. Lovers talk earnestly on park benches. Squirrels scuttle across your path. Pigtailed schoolgirls are conducted on nature

184

rambles in the sunshine. Eccentric vagrants eat sausage rolls out of grubby paper bags. Many a moody Coloured man shuffles meditatively between the elms. The long central avenue, pointing like a compass needle towards the mass of Table Mountain, is reserved for squirrels and pedestrians, and there is no garden path in Africa more conducive to sauntering or more instinct with the comforts of flirtation. Amiable Dutch buildings shine between its trees, and there are fountains here and there, and exotic flower-beds, and birds, and an easy mingling of races, black and brown and white and yellowish. This is the old vegetable garden of the Cape settlement, long ago mellowed and beautified; and it is astonishing to consider that each morning the Ministers of State walk through its genial delights, past the white synagogue and the art gallery, or briskly through the fallen leaves from Adderley Street, to enact the philosophies of apartheid.

Cape Town is a strangely delicate, maidenly city for a seaport and a capital, and what sense of power it has lies chiefly in its setting. It clusters most obscurely about the massif of Table Mountain, so that the poor stranger, already bewildered with politics and hospitality, never knows which direction he is facing, whether he is east or west of the great mountain, whether the sea is in front of him or behind, or which way he must walk to get home. Only the mountain stands firm, to re-assure him. It sits above the city in an attitude of righteous super-vision, stark but good, like a bewhiskered Victorian paterfami-lias in an antimacassared chair. If you drive down from Paarl early on a winter morning you may see its flat plateau protrud-ing brilliantly above the clouds that envelop the city, a sudden thin sliver of rock encouched in a cushion of white. At other times, if you stand on the green slopes of the mountain, you may observe the cloud resting soft as feather-down upon its plateau, while the Cape Town people jerk their thumbs affec-tionately at the old thing and say: 'Well, the tablecloth's spread this morning.' A huge cleft strikes diagonally across the north face of the mountain, and offers you an easy climb to the sum-mit. Heavenly beflowered slopes lead up to it, sprinkled with the spiky gaudy proteas; and there are pleasant little streams, and rocky grottoes, and a marvellous panorama of Table Bay below you. Nevertheless, the great plateau of Table Mountain, when at last you reach it, is a cold harsh place, inexplicably marine in flavour, and studded with little rock pools of rainwater, for all the world like some wide crab-scuttled beach in Cornwall. It has an ominous history. Climbers innumerable have been caught in the cloud up here, or lost their paths, or died of exposure. In the old days people used to be attacked by wild animals, and there are still snakes about and an occasional loathsome baboon. Some of these caves and crannies were once the refuges of escaped slaves, who made a practice of rolling boulders down the hill-side to discourage inquisitive passers-by. To this day the mountain claims its casualties; and sometimes, when a mist is rising, a blizzard threatening or a heavy damp cloud rolling in from the Atlantic, the gloomy wail of a siren warns the sight-seers that danger is on the way. Still, the view from Table Mountain is wonderful, the climb exhilarating, the cable railway giddying, and a notice on the summit urges you beguilingly to 'Keep Your Mountain Clean'.

There is a little of San Francisco to the city that rambles so incohesively about this mountain, and a whisper of France. This is an old and lenient capital. The fine white houses of the Dutch colonists still ornament its streets, and the castle is full of lovely Dutch furniture and pictures, a most comfortable, polished, gastronomic kind of fortress. There are flower-stalls (like Nob Hill) and Oriental quarters (like Chinatown) and down by the City Hall a jolly open-air market sets up its trestle tables and lures the passing sailor-men, and gives the city a trace of its old nautical roll. You can probably buy any-thing under the sun there, but I remember chiefly hundreds of thousands of obscure workshop tools and innumerable cluttered stalls of second-hand books. The crowd that oozes among these merchants is relaxed and friendly: and there are many of those absorbed shabby old men, *habitués* of markets everywhere, who seem to devote their old age to the worship of musty books, and who are to be seen there any morning devotedly buried in memoirs and mezzotints. Sometimes you may come across a soap-box orator in Cape Town, frothing a little at the mouth, spitting profusely and throwing himself about with stiff ungainly movements as he hoarsely declaims: 'Why, the Lord God, my friends, He knows, my friends, knows the innermost unspoken intimate thinkings and cogitations of your souls. My friends, He knows the ultimate machinations and considerations, my friends, of your ultimate beings, and He calls on you, calls on you now, my friends, calls on you before the Awful Day is here to think again, my friends, think again and cogitate and meditate and Repent!' I was once asked by a Coloured man outside the City Hall if I would like to buy a copy of *Lorna Doone*: and one day I saw the guest conductor of the Cape Town Symphony Orchestra striding through that market-place like a genie, wearing an imperial beard and a check tweed boiler-suit of his own design.

For Cape Town is an inconclusive, unregimented, individualist city, at least by the standards of the Union (not, by and large, a country for Sternes or Sir Richard Burtons). It makes allowances for mannerisms and minorities. Now and then, to prove the point, you may see a woman in a filmy blue dress and a veil, sidling through the back streets with a suggestion of the harem and a piquant trail of perfume. The Malays of Cape Town, descendants of slaves, bring the magic of Islam to the city and provide a soft Asiatic balm for its activities. On the doorsteps of their modest quarter you may see their doe-eyed children playing, squeaky but graceful; and there are little mosques with minarets and fairy lights; and proud old sages sitting in chairs in open doorways; and these modest billowing ladies, enshrouded in scent and sensibility. There is nothing gorgeously picturesque about the Malay quarter, nothing so bold and vivid as the big African locations, or so teemingly vigorous as the tenements of the coloured folk: but if you wander through these little streets, up and down these threadbare alleys, you will find yourself savouring the very smell of Islam, compounded of dust and red pepper and incense, and spiced with serenity.

It is partly sheer age that gives Cape Town its undertones of calm, and partly a measure of intellectual distinction, and partly (I like to think) its English associations. There are pleasant clubs overlooking squares, beside whose bars you may even, if you are lucky, bump into a professional actor (there are perhaps only four cities in the entire African continent where you may have this unexpected pleasure). There are bookshops innumerable, staffed by that particular kind of droopy-eyed lady to be found in staunchly democratic bookstores in the United States. There are Espresso coffee-shops, and prosperous book-lined suburbs, and the Mount Nelson Hotel, which is spattered with portraits of old English dignitaries, and apparently in-habited exclusively by dowagers and admirals of the White.

In short, I like Cape Town. Perhaps I have exaggerated its pleasures a little, and minimized its squalors, and touched up its colours a trifle, and rubbed away its smuts. You will probably not meet those actors in those bars. The guest conductor has long since gone home to Europe. The baboons of Table Mountain are almost extinct, and the perfumes of the Malayan ladies are, to be frank, apocryphal. But I owe the place a debt of gratitude, for I discovered that in Cape Town, alone among the South African cities, you can sometimes close your eyes to Nemesis: if you are as determined as steel, as frivolous as pink ribbon, as elusive as bath-soap, as bland as turtle-doves, you can actually dine out, from the *hors-d'oeuvres* to the Drakenstein brandy, without once discussing the Problems of Race. In the Union this is a sad little miracle: and thus, with a slightly fulsome bow to the Mother City, I gratefully acknowledge it.

ENVOI

Cynicism, disillusionment, shame, weariness, apathy—you may experience them all towards the end of a South African winter. The problems of this country are heart-rending, but can be a fearful bore, and even the honest hedonist may find himself frustrated in South Africa, and queerly troubled by his conscience. 'Ah well, it's not my fault, anyway,' he will assure himself as he uncorks another bottle, but somehow the disavowal rings obscurely false. We all share the guilt, or at least the failings, of white South Africa: each of us has his black Bantu, and we beat him every day.

Before you leave South Africa to pursue your own prejudices at home, drive away from Cape Town to the Cape of Good Hope itself, an invigorating windswept point at the tip of a heathland peninsula. Behind you the complacent mass of Table Mountain looms in grandeur, and the lights of the city flicker in the blue: in front there are only the seas, Atlantic to the west, Indian Ocean to the east. This is the extremity of Africa, one of those rare places where the very elements seem to be shaking hands in privacy. There is nothing but water between you and the Antarctic, nothing but land between you and Cairo.

Stifle the sententious thoughts that will certainly enter your mind, as you watch the waters mingle and the night seep in like soup. Stick to this simple principle: if there is sense to the turmoil of the tides below you, and the endless rotation of the days and nights, then there is sense to the tragedies and melancholies of South Africa. (But God only knows, observes the hedonist, inspecting the cheeses—the good Lord only knows what it is.)

INDEX

Africans, British, *see* British Africans

African natives: as prison labourers, *see* Farm prisons: in reserves, 94–6; *see also* Bantus, Compounds, Locations, Shanty-towns

African National Congress, 14, 127, 133, 135

Afrikaans, 46–7, 54, 66, 149; *see* Speech and Language

Afrikanderdom, 78–86

Afrikaners: agrarian, 48 seqq; of Bloemfontein, 64 seqq.; 'Boer' spirit of, *see* Boer, Pretoria; intellectuals among, 87–93; liberals among, 125; national character of, 13, 14, 79–86, *see also* Nationalists; 'poor whites' among, 82–3; and reserves, 94–6; sadism of, 52, 112; with tendencies toward fascism, 181; unenlightened background of certain, 91–2; Zulus, Indians, etc., and, 107–8

Alcohol, 25, 31, 32, 36, 49, 58, 66, 149, 179

Anglo-American Corporation, 19, 72, 73, 156–7, 174

Apartheid, principal references to, 15, 19, 23–9, 82, 131, 139–46, 161–7, 170–1, 176–83; and Boer wars, 45–6; basis of, in Baaskap and Calvinism, 91; clergy (Afrikaner) opposing, 92; European liberties and, 122, 179; intellectual life and, 87–93; liberalism (the more realistic) and, 129–36; liberalism's nebulous answer to, 126–7, 128, 129; Meadowlands move and, 128; nuances within, 139; Scriptures and, 144–5

Argus Press, 121

Association of Rand Pioneers, 49, 120

Attitudes, inter-racial and other: Afrikaner toward coloured people, 15, 37–8, 40, 50–5, 81–2, 85, 132–6; *see* Apartheid, Locations *and* related themes; Afrikaner toward English, 13, 14, 46–7, 69, 80–1, 83, 84; in Kruger tradition, 42–6; European, 13, 117–24; toward Indians, 107–8; 'twilight of democracy, 176–83; of intellectuals, 87–93; Jo'burg 'schizophrenia', 23 seqq.; of mine owners, 56–63; toward miscegenation, 161–7; parliamentary, 168–75, 176; of religious denominations, 53–5, 65–6; and reserves, 94–6; 'Slegs Blankes', 113–16; in Western Cape, 147–52. *See also* Boers, Liberals, Natal

Autocracy, 176–83

Baaskap, 14, 112, 122, 142, 161, 171–2; liberals and, 128

Baca tribe, Natal, 60

Bailey, Abe, 120

Baker, Sir Herbert, 41

Bandung bloc, 175

Bantus, 111–13, 140; as 'commodities', 112–13; numbers of, 111; 'Bantu areas' theory, total apartheid, 94–6

191

INDEX

INDEX

INDEX

Laws, repressive, 31–3; *see* Curfew, *also* Alcohol, Locations

Liberalism and Liberals, 125, 126–8, 129–36; of British South Africans, 122–5; true role of, 130–1

Libraries, public, 93

Ligers (lion-tiger cross), 67, 162

Locations, 23–4, 28–9, 30, 31, 34, 35–9, 41, 50–1, 63, 132, 133, 134, 179; of Durban, 109; of Johannesburg, 23–4, 28–9, 30, 50–1, 63; of Pretoria, 41; riots in, 110–11

'Long Cecil' (gun), 154

Louw, E., 171, 174–5

Luthuli, Chief, 27

Maize beer, 36; *see* Kaffir beer

Manchester Guardian, 93, 126, 177

Marais, Dr. Ben, 91, 92

Matabele, 44

Meadowlands, 31, 34, 59, 116, 128, 136

Mehlomakulu, Queen, 165

Mholo community, 97–8

Milner, Lord, 119

Mining, 19, 56–63, 71–8, 119, 153–60; compounds, 57–63; *and see* Kimberley

Miscegenation, 161 seqq.; and brothels, 164; illegality of, 165; in Ghana and Nigeria, 165

Missionaries, 95–6

Moroka, 34

Mount Nelson Hotel, Cape Town, 188

Mozambique, 60

Natal, 105, 106, 107, 117, 119, 147, 181

'National Constitution' (document), 182

Nationalist Party: as Broederbond shield, 170–2, 175; and democracy, 177–8, 180; Senate 'packing' by, 162–3, 180

Native Laws Amendment Bill, 179

Naval Hill Nature Reserve, Bloemfontein, 67

Navy, South African, 47, 107

New Age, 27

New Brighton, Port Elizabeth, 132, 133, 134, 136

New Delhi, 107

Newspapers, opposition, 92

Nylstroom, 119

Odendaalsrus, 72–8

Oppenheimer, E. and H., 74, 157, 174

Orange Free State, 64–70, 71–8, 81, 119, 147, 153, 155; rustic wedding in, 69–70; uranium in, 76–8

Orange growing, 48, 51

Orlando, 31, 34, 36–9, 59

Ossawa Brandweg, 181

Oxen, battle, 44

Paarl, 148, 149

Parliament, description and assessment of, 168–75, 184

Passports, 176, 178

Perestrello, 105

Pimville, 34

Pioneer free-and-easiness, survivals of, 114–16

Police, 25, 32, 37–8; brutality of certain, 112; 'police state', 176–83

Pondos, 94, 97, 127

'Poor whites', 82–5

Port Elizabeth, 132–8; as breeding-ground of Nationalism, 133; snake park at, 132, 133

Pretoria, 40–7, 168, 179; described, 40–1; Raadsaal at, 41–2

Proteas, on Table Mountain, 186

Rand, the, 115, 119, 153, 157

'Randocrats', 120

Randfontein, 56

Reef, the, 56–7, 111

Reeves, the Rt. Rev. Ambrose, 91

INDEX

Reitz, Denys, 86, 87
Rembrandt Tobacco Combine, 133
Reserves, the, 94 seqq.
Rhodes, Cecil, 14, 119, 120, 148, 153, 154, 155, 156, 157
Rickshaw men, Durban, 104

Segregation, Stellenbosch and, 139 seqq.
Shanty-towns, 30, 34, 35, 36
Shebeens, 32
Shuffle-dancers, 60-1
Sjambock, 112
Smuts, General, 79, 87, 131
Snake park, Port Elizabeth, 132, 133
Sophiatown, 31, 32, 33, 34, 128, 164, 182
South African Bureau of Racial Affairs (S.A.B.R.A.), 139, 140, 141
Speech and language (*see also* Afrikaans), 22, 30, 32-3, 169-70, 173-4, 181; and educational laws, 180
Splinter groups, 171
Springs, 17, 38, 56
Star, The (Johannesburg), 25
Stark, Freya, 136
Stellenbosch, 139-46, 147; unreality of planning by, 141, 142
Stevenson, Adlai, 172-3
Stinkwood, 65, 168
Strijdom, Mr., 170
Strikes, 37-9
Sugar, Durban-grown, 106
Suppression of Communism Act, 178
Swart, Dr., 170
Swaziland, 95; British detach from Transvaal, 119; Swazis, 60

Table Bay, Table Mountain, 185-6, 188
Tanganyika diamonds, 153
Telephone tapping, 137, 179
Tembas, 94, 97

'Tot' system, 150-2
Transkei, 115, 127; a trip across, 98-102; reserve, 83
Transvaal, 17, 79, 147, 153; property laws in, 33; rural, 48 seqq.
Treason trials, Johannesburg, 25-6, 108, 178
Tribal reserves, 94-104
Tribalism, preservation of, 34-5, 36, 56-7, 94-102, 135
Tsotsis, 23, 32, 37
'Twin streams' policy, 87, 131

Umtata 'Round Table', 98
Union Party, 131
United Party, 122, 125, 172-4, 175
Universities Apartheid Bill, 88, 179
Universities, the inter-racial, 87; *see also* Witwatersrand; the new 'State', 87-8
Uranium, 76, 77

Veldt described, 64
Verwoerd, Dr., 132, 171, 176
'Volk' concept, 84, 85, 92, 120, 133, 170, 176, 180
Volkslas Bank, 121
Volkswil, 47, 83; *see* Boer values
Voortrekkers, 43-5, 64, 118, 119; the Voortrekker Monument, 41-2, 68

Waratah (liner), 104
Welkom township, 73, 74
Whaling (Durban), 105
'Wild Coast', 97
Wine-Growers' Co-operative, 148, 149
Wine-growing, 148-52
Witch-doctoring, 98-101
Witwatersrand, 17, 71-2; gold reef, 56-7, 111; University, 24-5
Women's Monument (Orange Free State), 68

Xosas, 94, 97, 98, 99

195

INDEX